Healers of the Wild

People Who Care for Injured and Orphaned Wildlife

Donna Clement

FOR ALL CHAMPIONS OF THE WILD!

Shannon K. Jacobs

Coyote Moon Press
Denver, Colorado

Cover Photo by Gary Crandall

Photo Caption: *Dear Hearts*. Rehabilitators Cec and Tom Sanders (Wet Mountain Wildlife Rehabilitation Sanctuary in Florence, Colorado) feed orphaned fawns using Tom's invention, the MFF (Multiple Fawn Feeder).

Cover Design by Nancy Lund

About the Author: Shannon K. Jacobs grew up in New Mexico, where a life-long passion for wildlife and respect for indigenous cultures were rooted. She is the author of *The Boy Who Loved Morning* and *Song of the Giraffe*. She writes about what she loves — wild animals, wild places, native peoples, and those who cherish and protect them.

Published by

Coyote Moon Press
PO Box 6867
Denver, CO 80206
USA

Library of Congress Catalog Card Number: 97-094757
Jacobs, Shannon K.,
Healers of the Wild/ Shannon K. Jacobs — 1st ed.
Includes bibliographical references and index.

ISBN 0-9661070-0-4

I came on my sister alone and afraid
  It seems that she fell from the sky.
The gift that had carried her into the clouds
  Now was gone and she couldn't know why.

She'd sailed like a ship upon oceans of air,
  As wild and as free as the wind.
But something had taken her out of the sky,
  And now here to the earth she was pinned.

Come with me, my love, and we'll do what we can
  To set right what has somehow gone wrong.
We'll work with the feather and sinew and bone,
  To give back to your spirit its song.

From "Wild Again" © 1985 Douglas Wood
(complete lyrics on page 197)

Acknowledgments

I am deeply grateful to the many people who helped me create and produce this book. First and foremost is my husband, **George Jackson**. His patient and gracious support made this book possible.

A special thanks to **Elaine Thrune**, National Wildlife Rehabilitators Association president and wildlife rehabilitator (Wild Again in St. Cloud, Minnesota). In spite of her wildly hectic schedule, Elaine devoted many hours to reviewing and editing various stages of this book and advising me about important details of wildlife rehabilitation.

I also am indebted to:

Wildlife rehabilitators and related professionals who shared information in person, over the phone, or via mail. I couldn't feature everyone in the book but used all their information. They are: Susan Ahalt, Susan Andres, Becky Barron, Elizabeth Borden, Deborah Carr, Sandy Cate, Coleen Doucette, Bobbi Geise, Anna Gold, Kathy Green, Dick Griffin, Ralph Heath, Ed Hiestand, Nancy Houda, Kay Howell, Sue Howell, John Huckabee DVM, Joan Hughes, Catherine Hurlbutt, Diane Johnson, Shirley Kendall, Jessica Lainson DVM, Amanda Lollar, Sally Maughan, Shannon Mayo, Mark Mazzei, Lynne McCoy, Anne Miller, Megan Mosby, Penny and Jack Murphy, Lisa Rhodin, Phylis Rollins, Cec and Tom Sanders, Diana Schaffer, Tammie Scheich, Ellen Schultz, Dale Shields, Dawn Smith, Anne Steinmetz, Jo Ann Stoddard, Elaine Thrune, Rick Trout, Sigrid Ueblacker, Karen Von den Deale, Janet Walker, and Dave and Mary Young.

Illustrators and photographers, many of whom generously donated the use of their works in this book. (Their names and backgrounds are listed in the last section.) Gary Crandall's cover photo perfectly depicts wildlife rehabilitators.

Professional consultants, especially Maripat Murphy. Her editing expertise and copy-editing skills helped me shape and refine the book out of mountains of research. I would have destroyed my computer trying to learn desktop publishing without the assistance and knowledge of Karen Saunders. Paula Nicholas' illustrations made Chapters 20-22 come alive. Nancy Lund, graphic artist, created a masterpiece of a cover.

Readers of the manuscript at various stages gave me excellent feedback: Caroline Brawner, Lyn Carr, Catherine Hurlbutt, Valerie Kittel, Janine Lesser, Maripat Murphy, Penny and Jack Murphy, John Murray, Paula Nicholas, Cec and Tom Sanders, Elaine Thrune, Sigrid Ueblacker, Cindy Walker, and Sue and Wade Yenowine.

Life-sustaining listeners and information sharers: Amy Bevis, Brad Bowles, Irene Clurman, John Craiger DDS, Mary Crawford, Nancy and Greg Ewert, Paula Fox, Susan Geissler, Barb Gelhaar, Linda Hogan, Trisha Hood, Peggy and Michael Kappy, Brian and Jo Kittel, Virginia and Dale Kittel, Theresa Lowry, Desiree Cheri Nanette, John Nichols, Robin Perin, Alita Pirkopf, John Powers, Cindy Rork, Sheryl Scheller, Sherri Tippie, Betty Uptagraft, Jacki Wallace, Jesse White, and Marie Wittwer. Also, 4th-6th grades at Washington School Open Classroom in Salt Lake City (teacher Carolyn Turkanis); the 4th grade at Bishop Elementary in Englewood, Colorado (teacher Cindy Rork); and 3rd-5th grades at Ellis Elementary in Denver (teachers Sally Bell and Teri Appell).

Table of Contents

Why a Book About Wildlife Rehabilitators?

When I found a sick robin in my flower bed a few years ago, I had no idea what to do. Should I take it inside? Leave it alone? I asked family, friends, and neighbors for advice, but no one could help me.

Finally someone gave me the name of a wildlife rehabilitator. When I called and explained the problem, she asked me to take the bird to her home.

The rehabilitator gently examined the bird, then placed it in a box to rest. She said the bird probably had eaten insects sprayed with pesticides. Although she wasn't sure the robin would live, she promised to give it the best care possible. I left a donation before heading home, grateful for her help.

Later, I asked others what they knew about wildlife rehabilitators. No one knew anything. That was when I decided to write this book.

It's horrible to hear about the cruel and careless things people do to animals, but it's wonderful to learn about the people who help. Rehabilitators are the most remarkable group of people I've ever known. They are my heroes.

Their greatest (and often only) reward is to watch a wild animal go free, knowing they helped make it possible. By offering wildlife a second chance, these healers save a piece of wild for other generations of life...all life.

About This Book

This book describes what some wildlife rehabilitators do. It tells a few of their stories, describes some animals they care for, and recommends what you can do if you find injured or orphaned animals.

Words in italics are found in the glossary at the end of the book. Also included is information on how you can help wildlife rehabilitators.

Please do all you can to help.

Foreword

This book is a godsend for everyone who loves and respects wildlife and hates to see them suffer! People who read this book — both adults and kids — will learn how to help orphaned or injured wild animals. They will be able to react correctly and legally to a situation until a wildlife rehabilitator can be contacted.

For more than twenty years, wildlife rehabilitators have answered hundreds of thousands of phone calls from people who want to know what to do when they find wildlife in trouble. People's compassion for each animal is heartwarming. Sometimes, it is what keeps us going through trying times.

Healers of the Wild describes many wildlife rehabilitators of today — who we are, what we do, and a little about why we do what we do. No longer is it enough to mean well and have good intentions. We now share the knowledge to provide *proper* medical care, housing, nutrition, captive management, and release conditioning. We strive to respect and preserve the wildness of those entrusted to our care.

There is no other book quite like this one! Shannon's easy-to-read style weaves together stories, photographs, facts and advice. The stories and photographs are about real wild animals that have been helped by many dedicated volunteers and caring people working together across the United States. Since these stories are about real-life happenings, some are happy and some are sad. The facts and information help explain the situations — the causes, reasons, actions, and results.

When we realize some of the problems that wild animals face, we can help *prevent* injuries, poisonings, and orphaned youngsters. The more we understand wild creatures, the more we respect them and want to help them. The more we learn, the better we can help them. Those who understand wild ones will be able to tell when a rescue is necessary. Just as important, they will know when a rescue is *not* necessary.

The advice in this book will help everyone, especially kids, know what to do when they see a wild animal in trouble. Kids should not handle wild animals, but this books tells what kids *can* do to help.

Charts at the end of the book guide us through the thought process of determining what to do when finding an injured or orphaned baby bird or mammal. Other valuable resources include lists of wildlife rehabilitation organizations, state and federal agencies, and suggested books and videos.

We all want to do what is best for wild animals we encounter. Each injured or orphaned wild creature found by a person who reads this book will have a better chance of surviving and being returned to the wild where it belongs.

Thank you, Shannon.

Elaine Thrune, President
National Wildlife Rehabilitators Association

Who Helps Wildlife?

Heart of Gold. *These orphaned ducklings are among the hundreds of birds Anna Gold (Thornton, Colorado) rehabilitates every spring and summer.*

Chapter 1

What's Your Wildlife IQ?

WHAT WOULD YOU DO IF YOU...

- Mowed over a nest of baby bunnies in your yard?
- Discovered a raccoon family living in your attic?
- Found a fawn curled up alone in a meadow?
- Spotted a baby bird hopping in your flower bed?

These are familiar meetings between people and wild animals. Many people aren't sure what to do. Are you?

"I would take the animal home."

First, know that it's *against the law* to take wild animals home. Also, picking up wild animals often can harm them more than help them.

"I would take the animal to my vet."

Did you know that many veterinarians can't or won't treat wild animals? In some states, they must have special licenses to do so.

Photo: Shannon K. Jacobs

Raccoon Rascals. *What would you do if you found these cute youngsters in the woods?*

"I would give the animal to a zoo."

Zoos rarely take wildlife. Usually they don't have room, and zoo officials worry about diseases that wildlife carry.

Who Helps Wildlife?

Thankfully, there are people all over the country who help. They are called *wildlife rehabilitators*. Sometimes, they are known as "rehabbers."

WILDLIFE REHABILITATORS

To *rehabilitate* means to restore to health. Wildlife rehabilitators rescue and rehabilitate sick, injured, and orphaned wildlife. They release healthy animals back to the wild.

Surprisingly, most rehabilitators are not veterinarians. They are musicians, teachers, nurses, homemakers, retired people, biologists, and bakers, among others.

Because they've had special training, rehabilitators know the best ways to care for wildlife. Sometimes, that means leaving an animal alone, instead of rescuing it.

Rehabilitators also know what wild animals need for food, housing, or medical treatment. They've developed the skills necessary to safely handle wild creatures, and they've learned how to keep wild animals wild.

Rehabilitators Needed

Why are rehabilitators necessary? Because wild animals are in trouble. More and more people are moving into wildlife *habitats* (places where animals live naturally).

When land is *developed* (cleared for houses, businesses, or farming), wildlife homes and foods are destroyed. Wild animals then become *displaced* (forced out of their homes), injured, orphaned, or killed.

Photo: Shannon K. Jacobs

Displaced. Sandy Cate, Director of Adobe Mountain Wildlife Center in Phoenix, Arizona, holds a ring-tailed cat. It was accidentally dug out of its burrow by workers laying phone lines.

Wildlife Injuries

Rehabilitators estimate that 90% of the wild animals they treat are injured because of human activities.

The most common causes of wildlife injuries are collisions with man-made objects (cars, boats, airplanes, and windows), cat and dog attacks, shooting and trapping, poisoning, litter, and pollution.

**The Most Common Causes
of Wildlife Injuries**

- **Collisions with man-made objects (cars, boats, airplanes, windows)**
- **Cat and dog attacks**
- **Shooting and trapping**
- **Poisoning**
- **Litter/Pollution**

State Wildlife Agencies

Many people think that state wildlife officials or veterinarians are responsible for helping injured and orphaned creatures, but that's not true.

State wildlife agencies manage populations of wildlife. They don't take care of individual animals.

Veterinarians

Until recently, veterinarians weren't trained to treat wild animals at all. Now most veterinary schools offer some classes in wildlife medicine, but decent paying jobs in the field are rare.

Dr. John Huckabee is one of just a few wildlife veterinarians who work full-time in rehabilitation. He is director and staff veterinarian for Wildlife Center of Harris County Precinct 4 in Tomball, Texas.

"I went to veterinary school because I wanted to work with wildlife," Dr. Huckabee said.

"After graduation I moved to Houston. I was amazed to find no place for injured wildlife in the fourth largest city in the nation."

After trying for several years to start such a place, Dr. Huckabee was hired by Harris County to develop a wildlife center.

Today, the county supports the Center by paying the salaries for a veterinarian and veterinary technician. The county also funds the space in 320-acre Burroughs Park, office support, supplies and equipment, and utilities. Other money has to come from donations, grants, and volunteers.

Dr. Huckabee would like to see more county-supported rehabilitation centers. "We'd like to be a model for other counties that would like to do this," he said.

Photo: Jonathan X. Di Cesare

A Busy Schedule. *Dr. John Huckabee handles calls while examining a swamp rabbit scheduled for surgery. Dr. Huckabee is one of very few full-time wildlife veterinarians. Wildlife Center of Harris County Precinct 4 in Tomball, Texas, treats thousands of wild animals each year.*

FEATHERED, FURRED, AND SCALED

Some wildlife rehabilitators work with birds, mammals, and reptiles. A few specialize in certain creatures, such as bats, *raptors* (birds of prey), or *marine* (sea) animals.

Because so many wild creatures live around cities, a lot of rehabilitators take care of urban wildlife such as raccoons, foxes, skunks, opossums, and squirrels.

A small number of brave souls care for animals most of us would avoid — porcupines, bobcats, mountain lions, bears, and badgers.

Photo: Greenwood Wildlife Sanctuary

Prickly Porcupine. *A few brave souls take care of wildlife most people would avoid.*

Possum Passion

Like many rehabilitators, Phylis Rollins grew up loving animals. But that wasn't what nudged her into rehabilitation. It was her cat.

Early one morning, Phylis's cat caught a bird and turned it loose in her bedroom. Phylis spent hours trying to find help for the injured bird.

Finally she found a place that took wildlife, and she rushed the bird there. A volunteer admitted it to the center. Although very impressed with the place, Phylis didn't give it much more thought.

The next Sunday, her cat brought her another feathered trophy. Promptly returning to the center, Phylis handed over the second bird.

This time she also filled out an application to volunteer. It was her first step toward becoming a rehabilitator (and the last time her cat brought home a bird).

Phylis worked at the wildlife center once a week. She fed baby animals and cleaned cages.

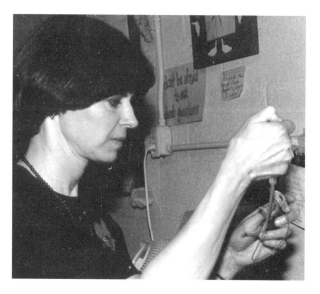

Photo: Phylis Rollins

Baby Food. *As a volunteer rehabilitator, Phylis Rollins learned to tube-feed baby opossums.*

16

Just when Phylis was wishing for more challenging work, the center admitted a mother opossum that had been badly tangled in a barbed-wire fence. She didn't live, but four of her babies did.

After the babies were cleaned up, the director asked Phylis to take care of them, so she did. That sparked Phylis's passion for opossums. She learned everything possible about the marvelous *marsupials* (pouched mammals).

Photo: Phylis Rollins

Jaws. *Phylis took care of a car-hit opossum named Jaws, whose mouth was wired shut temporarily, to allow the fractured jaws to heal.*

Soon she became the opossum team leader, responsible for training other volunteers as well as rescuing, rehabilitating, and releasing opossums.

Because of her other work rescuing turtles and tortoises, Phylis has been interviewed for television, radio, and newspapers — a big accomplishment for a very shy person.

BECOMING A REHABILITATOR

How do people become healers of the wild? Many begin as volunteers, like Phylis did, working with experienced rehabilitators and veterinarians.

State Permits

In most states, people must become licensed before they can rehabilitate wild animals on their own. This system ensures that people have the proper knowledge, skills, and facilities to care for wildlife. Volunteers, however, don't need permits, as long as they work at centers that are licensed.

States may require that rehabilitators pass courses in wildlife rehabilitation or prove their knowledge of wildlife, state laws, and handling of wild animals.

Sometimes, state wildlife inspectors visit homes to make sure people have correct cages, enclosures, and equipment, as well as veterinary help.

Beginners may have to work for a certain period of time with experienced rehabilitators.

Federal Permits

In order to rehabilitate *migratory* birds (those that fly between two habitats, spring and fall), rehabilitators must have special permits. These are handled by the U.S. Fish and Wildlife Service (USFWS).

People who rehabilitate *endangered species* (animals threatened with dying off) also need special permits from USFWS.

The National Marine Fisheries Service (NMFS) oversees the rescue and rehabilitation of marine mammals. NMFS issues permits, which are called Letters of Authorization (LOA), to qualified centers.

Photo: Becky Barron

Dolphin Helper. *Lynne Stringer works with Noodge, a rough-toothed dolphin. Lynne is lead animal technician with Wildlife Rescue of the Florida Keys, a center with a permit from National Marine Fisheries Service to rescue and rehabilitate marine mammals.*

Photo: Heidi Bucknam

Silver Plume. *People who rehabilitate endangered species or migratory birds need special permits from the U.S. Fish and Wildlife Service.*

The centers must prove that they have experienced staff and veterinary help, proper equipment, an appropriate place to keep the animals, and money to pay for expenses.

Kids Want to Know

Q: How many rehabilitators are there?

A: About 5,000 wildlife rehabilitators are licensed by states. New York has the most, with 680. Alabama and West Virginia do not license rehabilitators. Alaska licenses only bird rehabilitators.

Q: How many wild animals are helped by rehabilitators?

A: Every year, hundreds of thousands of wild creatures are helped directly. Indirectly, rehabilitators assist millions more by educating people about wildlife issues and helping them deal with human-wildlife conflicts *humanely* (in a kind manner).

They also work very hard to preserve wildlife habitats.

Q: Who pays rehabilitators?

A: Most are not paid for their work at all. In fact, they often pay out of their own pockets for food, cages, and medicines. That's why a lot of rehabilitators form nonprofit organizations — so they can ask for donations from people and companies.

Photo: Shannon K. Jacobs

Nonprofits. *Many rehabilitators form nonprofit wildlife organizations, such as this one in Key West.*

If your family donates money, equipment, or supplies to a nonprofit wildlife rehabilitation group, you can deduct it from taxes (parents really like that).

Q: How much does it cost to rehabilitate wildlife?

A. A lot. One raptor rehabilitator estimated that she spends $350 to return one bird of prey to the wild.

Another healer who cares for birds, mammals, and reptiles pays about $8,000 a year for wildlife expenses.

Costs for rehabilitating one orphaned harbor seal pup can run up to $1,500.

Photo: Caroline Brawner

Harbor Seal Pup. *It can cost as much as $1,500 to raise and release one orphaned baby seal.*

Q: What do the expenses include?

A: Food, housing, medical supplies, and veterinary care. Also included are rents or leases, insurance, phones, vehicles, gas, electricity, and heating.

Sometimes rehabilitation centers receive donated items from companies, such as dog food from pet stores, fruits and vegetables from grocery stores, or building supplies from lumber companies. These donations save them thousands of dollars a year.

Some average costs and hospital days at Greenwood Wildlife Rehabilitation Sanctuary in Longmont, Colorado:

Baby bird:	$1 a day for 30 days
Baby rabbit, squirrel, or prairie dog:	$2 a day for 40 days
Baby fox, coyote, or raccoon:	$3 a day for 120 days

Q: How do rehabilitators learn how to care for wild animals?

A: They get a lot of hands-on experience, and they share information among themselves. They also take classes, attend conferences and workshops, and constantly read books and articles about wildlife biology and treatment.

Two national organizations — National Wildlife Rehabilitators Association (NWRA) and International Wildlife Rehabilitation Council (IWRC) — provide classes for beginners and experienced rehabilitators. State wildlife rehabilitation associations also offer continuing education courses.

Q: How much time does it take to rehabilitate wildlife?

A. It takes a lot of time and a very serious commitment, especially during the wild and crazy times of the year, such as spring and summer. Anyone interested in becoming a rehabilitator should talk it over with (and volunteer with) experienced people.

Photo: Greenwood Wildlife Rehabilitation Sanctuary

Feed Me! Feed Me! *It takes a lot of time and energy to rehabilitate wildlife. They need frequent feedings, warmth, attention, companionship with their own species, proper enclosures, and thorough survival training.*

Rescue – The First Step

Wet and Wild. Volunteers from The Marine Mammal Center (left to right) Vi Brown, Guthrum Purdin, and Rebecca Duerr rescue California sea lions entangled in fishing nets. They take the sea lions to safer ground, remove the nets, and release healthy animals. If badly injured, the sea lions may be admitted for treatment.

Chapter 3

Anyone Can Help

Daylight Urban Owl

"Hey, look, an owl!" a man in downtown Denver cried. He pointed to a crosswalk signal. Upon it sat a beautiful great horned owl.

All morning, people on their way to work stopped to stare at the bird. Television reporters arrived in the afternoon to film the urban owl for the evening news.

Finally, someone got worried about the bird and called the Colorado Division of Wildlife. The Division contacted Birds of Prey Foundation.

Michael Judish, a volunteer trained in raptor rescue, quickly showed up to help. He explained to the crowd that the bird wasn't behaving normally.

"Owls should avoid people," he said. "Something's wrong when a wild animal lets you get this close."

To prove his point, Michael stepped up next to the raptor. The bird didn't move away or turn around. That made its capture easy.

Michael wore gloves to pick up the bird so the owl wouldn't *foot* (slash) him with its *talons* (sharp claws).

Photo: Critter Alley

Footing Protection. It's important to wear gloves when handling birds of prey. Even young ones, such as this great horned owl, can slash with their talons.

When Birds of Prey Foundation Director Sigrid Ueblacker examined the owl (named StopGo), she discovered why he'd put up with crowds of people and screeching traffic — he was blind. StopGo probably had collided with a car while hunting a mouse.

StopGo's head injury was temporary, though. The owl completely recovered and was released a few weeks later.

EXPERIENCE NOT NEEDED

You don't have to be an experienced rescuer to assist wildlife; anyone can help. For kids, the most important thing to do is *get an adult right away*. What should adults do? Call a wildlife rehabilitator.

If someone had contacted Birds of Prey Foundation as soon as StopGo was spotted downtown, the owl would have been rescued immediately.

Rehabilitators recognize abnormal behavior in animals. They know when it's important to capture the animals quickly, for people's safety as well as the animals'.

Rehabbers give the best advice on when to rescue and when *not* to. This helps to prevent the many unnecessary rescues that happen with young animals.

BABY-NAPPERS

Did you know that very few baby animals are true orphans? Unfortunately, kindhearted people often pick up baby animals, thinking they need help.

Without a background in the *natural history* (habits, biology, and needs) of wildlife, most of us aren't able to make good judgments about them.

If you saw a baby bird hopping on the ground, for example, you might think it was an orphan. But, probably it would be a *fledgling* (young bird learning to fly). Sometimes, you can identify fledglings by their short tail feathers, *down* (fuzz) on their heads, and clumsy movements.

While practicing flying skills, fledglings spend several days hopping around on the ground. Normally their parents are nearby, feeding and caring for the young birds until they can find their own food.

> **Fledglings need help only if they are sick or injured, or if cats, dogs, or people are a threat to them.**

Photo: *Karen Von den Deale*

Fuzzy-headed Fledglings. *These oriole youngsters are learning how to fly. Their parents still feed them.*

Out of Sight, *Not* Out of Mind

Because they look so helpless, fawns and baby seals get rescued a lot. People don't understand that it's normal behavior for these creatures to lie quietly in grass or on a beach and wait for their mothers. Usually the mothers are feeding nearby.

Photo: Critter Alley

Mom Knows. *A fawn's lack of scent protects it from predators.*

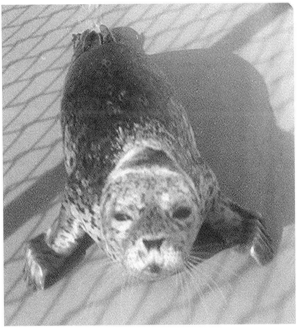

Photo: Caroline Brawner

Don't Rescue Me. *Most baby seal rescues are unnecessary, because the mothers have not abandoned their young. They are feeding close by.*

Fawns' spotted coats help them blend in with bushes and grass so *predators* (animals that hunt and eat other animals) can't see them. Fawns usually don't have a scent, so predators can't smell them.

If you pick up a healthy baby, you are taking it away from its best chance for survival— its mother.

Fawns and seal pups need help only if they are crying, injured, or in danger from predators, or if you know for sure the mother is dead.

Home, Sweet Home

Family reunions do happen, even when baby animals are rescued by mistake. But they take a lot of time and energy.

For instance, when a woman rescued 10 baby ducklings crossing a busy street in Boulder, Colorado, she also tried to capture the mother duck.

She couldn't catch her, so she took the babies to Greenwood Wildlife Rehabilitation Sanctuary. It was a good thing the woman remembered exactly where she'd picked up the babies. Elaine Myers, an animal care coordinator at Greenwood, immediately took the ducklings back to where they'd been rescued and searched for the mother.

Greenwood already had 22 baby ducklings in the intensive care unit. Ten more would have tipped the scales.

Photo: Shannon K. Jacobs

Sitting Ducks. Keeping mom and her young together is very important.

When Elaine saw two mallard ducks paddling down the nearby creek, she held up the box of peeping babies, hoping they were the parents. They weren't. Two more mallards floated by, and Elaine again showed off the fuzzy ducklings.

"Quack!" cried the female duck, slowly approaching the babies.

Elaine set down five ducklings, and the female duck herded them into the creek. She then released the rest of the ducklings. They swam wildly to catch up with their mother and siblings, peeping in their high-pitched voices. Finally, the reunited family floated off. Father mallard stayed in the back, to make sure no babies strayed.

Pellet Clues

In another case in Scottsdale, Arizona, five owl babies (from three different families) were rescued and brought to Liberty Wildlife Rehabilitation Foundation — all in one week. The owlets were healthy, so Liberty volunteer Peggy Kavookjian made it her mission to return them to their nests.

How did Peggy find the nests? She returned to where the babies were rescued and looked for *owl pellets* under trees.

Mystery Clues?
Owl pellets.

Photo: Shannon K. Jacobs

Owls spit up the pellets, which are made of fur, teeth, and bones that haven't been digested. If a family of owls *roosts* (rests or sleeps) in a tree, sausage-shaped pellets can be found under it.

Following pellet clues, Peggy found a palm tree with an adult owl in it. She left the baby owl in nearby bushes. When she checked back the next day, she saw the fledgling sitting next to its parent.

Three other *nestling* (unfeathered, still in the nest) owls had fallen from their damaged nest, which was located inside the arm of a saguaro cactus! Using a ladder to climb the tall, bristly cactus, Peggy and her husband repaired the nest. Then they returned the baby owls to their rebuilt home under the watchful eyes of the mother owl.

The final owlet had been found on someone's property. Peggy and the owner walked the land, searching for owl clues. When they spotted pellets under a tree, they also saw the nest. Peggy left the fledgling at the bottom of the owl tree where the parents would find it.

This was a lot of work for Peggy, but it was well worth it. Young owls are raised best by their parents.

LOVING WILDLIFE TO DEATH

Some people rescue wild creatures by taking them home. They think they can care for the animals properly because they love them.

But love is not enough. Caring for wild animals is very different from raising cats and dogs. Ignorance about their needs causes permanent injuries, suffering, and death.

Photo: Karen Von den Deale

Deformed Bluejay. *This young bird was raised illegally in someone's home and fed the wrong diet, which caused its bone deformity. The bird had to be put to sleep.*

Imagine if you were hurt in a car accident. Would you want someone off the street, with no medical background, taking you home? Or would you want help from a medical expert in a hospital? It's no different with wildlife. They deserve the best professional care possible.

Photo: Critter Alley

Where's Mom? *These orphaned raccoons will get the best care possible at a rehabilitation center.*

> **It's against the law in most states to keep wild animals without permits, even if you plan to release them.**

These laws were created to protect animals from people who steal them, sell them, or who harm them by taking them home. They also were created to protect public health. Wild animals carry diseases and *parasites* (fleas, ticks, lice, or worms).

Finding Wildlife Rehabilitators

It's a good idea for everyone — families, schools, businesses, and community organizations — to keep a list of nearby wildlife rehabilitators.

Call or write your state wildlife agency and ask for the names of rehabilitators who care for birds and mammals. Sometimes, one person will handle both.

State wildlife agencies are listed alphabetically in the last section of this book.

If there are no rehabilitators in your town or city ... Ask your state wildlife agency to give you the name of the *nearest* rehabilitator. Even if that person is a few hundred miles away, he or she can give you advice over the phone if you call for help.

If you're traveling in another city or state ... Call the state wildlife agency listed in the phone book. You also can check the yellow pages for "Wildlife Rescue" or "Animal Shelter."

If rehabilitators are not listed in a phone book ... Call any of these places and ask for the nearest wildlife rehabilitator:

- Humane Society
- Audubon Society
- Wild Bird Centers or
  Wild Birds Unlimited
- City Animal Control Officers
- Veterinarians (wildlife/exotic)
- Highway Patrol
- Coast Guard or Marine Patrol
- U.S. Fish and Wildlife Service
  (for migratory birds)

UNTIL YOU REACH A REHABBER

If you find an animal that looks injured or orphaned, observe the animal carefully, then ask an adult to call a rehabilitator before any other action is taken.

If the rehabilitator decides that the animal needs help, she or he will arrange for its rescue, either picking up the animal or asking a volunteer (maybe the caller) to take it to a rehabilitation center.

Anyone who decides to help with a rescue should always consider his safety first. Frightened wild animals bite, scratch, kick, or stab.

Rehabilitators explain how to capture and handle animals safely. Special capture methods are used for different *species* (kinds) and ages of animals, as well as for specific situations.

No one should try to rescue an adult animal without guidance from a rehabilitator. Adult animals are too dangerous to handle without professional help.

30

How to Help Without Rescuing

If someone chooses not to rescue, there are other ways to help until rescuers arrive.

Sick or injured animals will try to hide in bushes, drains, or tall grass if they're able to move. If a person stays within sight of the animal, he can tell rescuers exactly where it's hiding.

Another way to help is to put a plastic laundry basket or cardboard box (with air holes) over the creature to keep it in one place. That will protect it from predators until help arrives.

For detailed steps on how to rescue baby birds and mammals, turn to *If You Find Orphaned or Injured Animals* in the next-to-last section of this book.

Photo: Catherine Hurlbutt

Ice-pick Sharp. *Rehabilitator Jean Lisle carefully holds an injured western grebe, a water bird known for its strong neck and lightning-fast stabs. (Untrained people should not rescue water birds without a rehabilitator's help. The birds can inflict serious wounds, including putting out an eye.)*

Photo: Catherine Hurlbutt

Ready to Roll. *A quick-thinking rescuer placed this mourning dove inside a soft drink container before calling a rehabilitator. This prevented the bird from flapping around and making its broken wing worse.*

31

Baby Bird Quiz

Question: Should this baby great horned owl be rescued? It's a fledgling that has left the nest. The parents are still feeding it.

Photo: *Michael Judish*

Answer: The bird does *not* need to be rescued. As long as it is safe from predators (including cats, dogs, and people), and the parents are feeding it, the young owl is okay.

Chapter 4

Kids Want to Know

Q: My brother brought home baby birds that fell out of their nest. What should we feed them?

A: Before you do anything (even feed them) ask an adult to call a rehabilitator or your state wildlife agency right away.

Don't wait a few hours or days. Young birds die quickly without the right care.

Photo: Karen Von den Deale

Get Help. *Baby birds need professional help. If you find baby birds, call a rehabilitator.*

The rehabilitator will tell you what to do with the birds. If she asks your parents to put the baby birds back in their nest, she'll explain how to do that.

If the birds are injured or can't be returned to the nest, the rehabilitator may ask your family to take the birds to her.

Your brother was a hero for rescuing the baby birds that would have died without his help. Now your family needs to give the birds their best chance for survival — professional advice or care from a wildlife rehabilitator.

Q: I helped friends take a nest of squirrels to a rehabilitator. My mother said I shouldn't have carried the squirrels in my jacket. Why not?

A: Most wild animals have parasites. Some have diseases that can be passed to people and pets. That's why kids should never touch wild animals. Always let adults do the handling.

Photo: Critter Alley

Don't Handle Wildlife. *Most wild animals have fleas, lice, or ticks. They also carry diseases. That's why kids should never handle wild critters.*

Q: Do mother animals really reject their babies if people touch them?

A: We've all heard that, but it isn't true. Most birds have a poor sense of smell, so they can't tell when their babies have been touched by people. That's why it's okay to put baby birds back in their nests if they fall out (and if they aren't injured).

Mammals do have a good sense of smell, but mammal moms won't reject their babies if people handle them as *little as possible*.

For example, if your dad mowed over a nest of baby bunnies, he could repair the nest and replace the babies (if they weren't injured). The mother rabbit would keep caring for her babies, as long as people stayed away from the nest.

A lot of wild babies don't have scents when they're born. This protects them from predators. Too much touching, though, can leave a human scent. This might lead predators to the nest.

Q: My cousin picked up an injured bat and took it home. When the bat bit him, the department of health took the bat away to be tested for rabies. But they killed the bat! It didn't have rabies, so why did they kill it?

A: If a wild animal bites a person, it has to be checked for *rabies*. Rabies is a deadly viral disease that all warm-blooded animals — including humans — can get from an infected animal.

That's especially true if the animal is a coyote, bat, raccoon, skunk, or fox. These are *rabies vector species* (animals that most often get rabies and infect other animals).

Photo: Tom Sanders

Rabies Vector Species. *Coyotes, skunks, foxes, raccoons, and bats get rabies and infect others more often than other animals.*

Rabies can't be treated in animals, but it can be treated successfully in humans. If you know someone who has been exposed to rabies, *he should get to a doctor immediately*. If he waits until symptoms appear, it will be too late; he will die. Rabies is fatal without prompt treatment.

Photo: Urban Wildlife Rescue

Hands Off! *Never, never, never touch a wild bat. Only a tiny number of bats actually have rabies, but there is no way of knowing what's wrong with a sick or grounded bat.*

Checking for rabies requires killing animals that might have the disease. Why? Because samples of their brains are tested for the virus.

Never touch a wild bat, especially a bat on the ground. It's probably sick. Although only a tiny number of sick bats actually have rabies, it's impossible to tell what is actually wrong with a grounded bat.

**A bat can't hurt you
if you don't touch it.**

But if you pick it up, the bat may defend itself with its teeth. Then it will have to be killed and checked for rabies.

So if you want to save a bat, *don't handle it*. Notify an adult, and ask him or her to call your state wildlife agency.

If you know of a local rehabilitator who takes care of bats, ask the adult to call that person. People who rehabilitate bats are vaccinated against rabies, and they take precautions to avoid getting exposed to rabid animals.

Q: What should we do about turtles crossing roads? A lot get run over.

A: If you can do it safely, carry the turtle to the other side of the road. Just make sure you take it in the direction it was headed. Otherwise, it'll turn around and cross the road again.

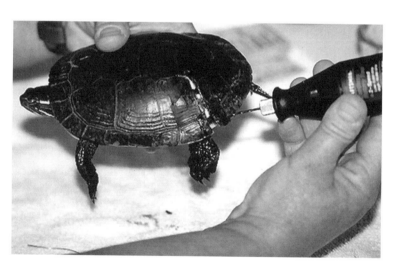

Photo: Critter Alley

Repairing Shell Damage. *Often a shell can be wired or glued back together after a turtle is run over by a car. But this is not a simple procedure. Only rehabilitators or veterinarians should do it. Infections and other injuries need to be treated as well.*

Q: My dad says we shouldn't worry about saving common animals like pigeons and opossums. Is he right?

A: "Nothing deserves to suffer," said Catherine (Birdie) Hurlbutt. "Every living creature deserves humane treatment."

A bird rescuer and former rehabilitator in Denver, Colorado, Birdie has devoted her life to helping wild creatures, especially birds. She is a legend in the Denver community.

"What would a child learn about compassion if she brought me a sick bird and I refused to help it, just because it was common?" Birdie asked.

Her mission is to show kids that adults really do care about wild creatures. During summers, Birdie drives many miles a day, sometimes up to 100, rescuing feathered friends. That's a lot of miles for an 84-year-old with an oxygen tank. That explains why her car has 310,000 miles on it!

Photo: Shannon K. Jacobs

Birdie. *Catherine Hurlbutt is a best friend to birds.*

Q: Is it fun to rehabilitate animals?

A: Taking care of wild critters definitely is fun, but only about half the time. The other half is not fun, because about 50% of the animals either die or are beyond help when admitted.

The work can be very difficult, tiring, and discouraging. Some rehabilitators "burn out." That means they've overdone it physically and emotionally. When that happens, they may have to cut back on animal patients or leave rehabilitation altogether for awhile.

Part of what new rehabbers learn is how to take care of themselves *and* find time and energy to cope with difficult decisions, demanding schedules, and lack of money.

The more the average person knows about wildlife rehabilitation, the more support rehabilitators will receive. This will help everyone, especially the wild critters they've devoted their lives to.

Photo: Urban Wildlife Rescue

Look at Me, Ma! *Wild critters, especially young ones, provide lots of laughs for rehabilitators. Critters' crazy antics help make up for hard work, emotional rough times, and no pay.*

Rehabilitation – The Second Step

Photo: Karen Von den Deale

Cat Attack. *This infant gray squirrel suffered a broken leg when attacked by a cat. Thankfully, the little critter was rehabilitated successfully and later released.*

Chapter 5

Hospitals for Wildlife

Admitting Wildlife

Many rehabilitation centers are home-based, meaning they're located in rehabilitators' homes and backyards. Others are like clinics, housed in separate buildings. A few centers are part of nature centers or universities.

An animal brought to a center is examined by a rehabilitator and given first aid, if needed.

Very young or chilled babies may go into *incubators* (enclosures with controlled heat and humidity) for warmth.

Newly admitted animals are *quarantined* (put in separate cages) to protect other animals from diseases the new patients might be carrying.

Rehabilitators keep a chart on each patient, just as in human hospitals.

Since volunteers often work in shifts, a person on each shift writes notes about the animals' conditions, feedings, treatments, and medications. This keeps everyone up-to-date.

Working With Veterinarians

Animals with diseases, broken bones, or internal injuries are taken to a veterinarian. If surgery is done, the animal is returned to the rehab center for recovery.

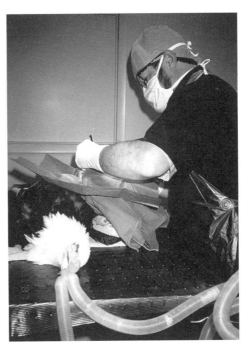

Photo: Sigrid Ueblacker

Generous Vets. Dr. Lee Eggleston operates on an eagle with a broken leg.

41

Some large centers have their own wildlife veterinarians. Most rehabilitators work with local veterinarians. These professionals often donate their services.

CRAFTING CAGES

When animals become well or old enough to take care of themselves, they're moved from indoor cages to outdoor enclosures. Several animals of the same species live together, getting used to each other and spending less time with humans.

Photo: Shannon Brink

Coons Keeping Cool. *Housing the same species together, such as these orphaned raccoons, helps them stay wild and learn from each other.*

Dangerous Wire Cages

Animals kept in the wrong kind of cages can develop serious or fatal injuries. Some sad examples are wild birds that rehabilitators get after they're *confiscated* (taken away by law enforcement officials) from people who capture them illegally.

These bird-nappers often keep the birds in wire cages, but wild birds aren't tame, and they don't sit quietly. They break bones and damage feathers, trying to escape.

Rehabilitators often keep tiny, newly hatched baby birds in berry boxes, margarine containers, or aquariums that are inside incubators for warmth. Older baby birds are put in cardboard or wooden boxes covered with a soft netting or in small, nonwire cages.

Stages of Recovery

Each stage of an animal's recovery requires different space. For instance, an owl with a broken wing might do better in a small, dark cage at first, where it can calm down and rest.

Later, with the wing healed, the owl might be moved to a *flight cage* (a specialized, large outdoor enclosure). There the owl could develop the muscle strength and coordination necessary for flying.

Photo: Sigrid Ueblacker

On the Mend. *A roomy flight cage enables a snowy owl to strengthen flying muscles.*

Photo: *Sally Maughan*

Orphaned Cubs. *Most of the black bears Sally rehabilitates are orphaned when their mothers are killed by hunters or hit by cars.*

Photo: *Sally Maughan*

Big Guys. *Large animals, such as these bears, need very strong enclosures.*

Good Old Bear

Some enclosures need to be very sturdy, especially if they hold large animals. Sally Maughan (Idaho Black Bear Rehab, Inc.) has spent about $3,500 of her own money to construct a strong main enclosure for adult bears and a pen for cubs.

Of the 27 bear cubs Sally has rehabilitated, most were orphaned when their mothers were hit by cars, killed during spring or fall bear hunts, or *poached* (hunted illegally).

When the cubs are brought to Sally, they may weigh only five pounds. By December, when they're ready to *den* (sleep) for the winter, the bears are as big as Sally and weigh 65-100 pounds!

During one busy year, Sally cared for 15 bears. The animals stayed in a chain link enclosure that was strong enough to support climbing cubs.

Sally entered the enclosure twice a day to feed the bears and clean up after them. The bears were fairly predictable, with one exception — Griz, the most powerful bear Sally had ever had.

One day, Griz grabbed Sally in a bear hug, holding her so tightly she couldn't move or turn. When Griz's sister distracted him, Sally escaped. Although she was frightened, Sally knew that Griz wasn't trying to hurt her. He just thought she was one of the bears.

Photo: Sally Maughan

Griz. *A powerful black bear, Griz dries off after his daily swim.*

Each November, Sally begins cutting back on the bears' food. She usually stops feeding them around Thanksgiving, so the sleepy bears will climb inside their dens for the winter, just as wild bears do.

The "dens" Sally provides are dog houses, dog kennels, large hollow logs, and a turned-over 160-gallon swim tub.

Later in the winter, Sally and wildlife officials move the sleeping bears to real dens in wilderness areas. The bears sleep there until spring, when they wake up wild and free.

Photo: Sally Maughan

Bear Den. *Shenandoah, an eight-month-old black bear rests in her hollow log den.*

44

MARINE ANIMALS

Enclosures for marine animals like otters, dolphins, whales, sea turtles, and seals require clean pools of water that are chemically balanced and kept at correct temperatures. Some need *haul-out areas* (places where the animals can climb out of the water), just like in the wild.

Because of these complicated housing needs, only specialized rehabilitation centers or aquariums are equipped to handle captive marine animals.

© 1997 The Marine Mammal Center / Photo: Jane Oka

Romping on the Ramp. *Steller sea lions, like all marine animals, need large enclosures in specialized centers.*

Crank Up the Heat

Keeping baby animals warm is critical for their survival. Rehabbers place heating pads, light bulbs, or hot water bottles in parts of cages so animals can seek warmth when they need it, or they can move away from it.

Photo: Catherine Hurlbutt

Choosing Heat. *A newly-hatched baby pheasant sits on top a hot water bottle, while a fully feathered house sparrow and kingbird (lower right) choose to stay away.*

Young animals die quickly from cold. One man learned this sad lesson when he rescued two baby sandpipers whose mother had been run over by a car.

He placed the baby birds in a big box and took them to a wildlife center. What went wrong? The man had put a wet beach towel in the box with the birds, possibly trying to cover or cushion them.

45

But the towel chilled the babies. They arrived at the center shaking with cold. Both birds died.

For steps on what to do for orphaned animals, turn to *If You Find Orphaned or Injured Animals* in the next-to-the-last section of this book.

Stressed OUT

Would you be frightened if huge creatures kidnapped you and locked you in a cage, then surrounded you, baring their sharp teeth and staring at you?

That's how we appear to captive wild creatures. They are terrified of us. Every time a human approaches, they fear for their lives.

Many wild animals die from the stress of captivity. Stress also slows down their healing processes.

That's why a veterinary hospital or animal shelter full of barking dogs is a terrible place to keep wildlife.

Rehabilitators try to keep animals in quiet places away from the human sights, sounds, and smells that panic them. They hang towels in front of cages to give the animals privacy, and they ask volunteers not to stare into the cages and to be quiet while working nearby.

Staring is very threatening to wild animals. It's what predators do to their prey.

Think how a cougar stalks a deer, staring at it from the high grass. Think how an eagle glares at a rabbit it plans to grab in its talons. When a human stares at a small animal, that creature thinks it's going to be eaten.

That's why, out of respect and understanding, rehabilitators avoid looking directly at animals when working inside or near their cages.

Photo: Greenwood Wildlife Rehabilitation Sanctuary

Hideaway. Rehabilitators make sure wild animals, such as these shy foxes, have places to hide from people. These lucky critters have a snug den within their enclosure.

Chapter 6

Roadkill Cafe

CARNIVORE CUISINE

Rehabilitators sometimes joke that their families won't go near their wildlife freezers. If you took a peek inside, you'd appreciate why wild food is stored separately from people food.

Wildlife freezers are jammed with meat-eaters' delights. Some wildly popular foods are "mouse-cicles" (frozen mice) which are supplemental foods for raptors, bobcats, coyotes, foxes, and vultures, among others.

Delicious when thawed and served whole, mouse-cicles can be skinned and chopped, blended, or whipped into a fabulous mouse mousse.

Fast Food

Other frozen treats are slabs of venison, sides of beef, or baggies stuffed with frozen rats, rabbits, quails, or chickens. Always recyclers, rehabilitators don't waste fresh meat, even roadkill. Whole animals (meat, fur, feathers, bones, and guts) are the best source of nutrients for wild *carnivores* (meat eaters).

Photo: Heidi Bucknam

Munched Mouse. *Regular fresh meat gives wild carnivores, such as this great horned owl, important nutrients in their diet. (Frozen food is only a substitute.)*

Creative Cooking

If you've ever lifted 20 pounds, then you know how much meat three cougar cubs gobbled *every day* at Wet Mountain Wildlife Rehabilitation Sanctuary in southern Colorado.

Photo: Tom Sanders

Costly Wild Cats. *These orphaned cougar cubs gobbled 20 pounds of meat every day while being rehabilitated. Typical of wild cats, the snarling cubs got up as high as they could — in this case onto a high platform inside their large enclosure — to get as far away from people as possible.*

The rehabilitators, Cec and Tom Sanders, tossed the snarling triplets wild meat — especially venison — when it was available. Otherwise, the three-month-old cubs wolfed down car-hit cottontails and other roadkill quickly scraped up by loyal volunteers.

It takes creativity to keep costs down. Many wild animals need meat, but the fresh and frozen stuff is expensive to buy.

Cutting Costs

A mouse or small rat can cost a dollar apiece. Multiply that by six to figure what a great horned owl typically eats a day.

Raptors in one rehabilitation center chow down on 25,000 mice a year!

To cut expenses, some centers raise their own colonies of rats, mice, rabbits, and quail to feed the wildlife. Many grow earthworms and *mealworms* (beetle larvae) as well.

Joan Hughes (Volunteers for Wildlife, Westbury, New York) keeps packets of smelts (small, silvery fish) in her freezer for seagulls.

"Gulls will eat anything in the wild," she said. "But in captivity, they want nothing but smelts."

Joan freezes blueberries for berry-loving birds like cedar waxwings. For insect-eating birds, Joan raises mealworms, but she also buys them live crickets and earthworms.

People in the community sometimes help out, too. When a California rehabilitation center became desperate for raptor food, fifteen 4-H clubs saved the day by trapping and freezing hundreds of rodents.

Occasionally, ranchers donate a dead (nondiseased) cow, or hunters haul in a freshly bagged antelope or elk.

One raptor rehabilitator claimed she learned to "quarter a road-killed deer in five minutes" to take advantage of fresh deer dropped off by wildlife officials.

LEARNING ABOUT WILD FOODS

Sick, orphaned, and injured creatures need good nutrition to heal and grow. Rehabbers spend a lot of time learning about the foods their wild patients eat in nature. They then teach the orphans about these foods. Otherwise, the young animals could starve after release.

Photo: Karen Von den Deale

Caught One! *A young kingfisher catches a fish in a dish. Rehabilitators must take the place of parents, teaching orphaned birds how to catch or find food.*

Dangerous Human Food

Human food can make baby animals sick enough to die. It often causes malnutrition. Some problems of malnutrition — weak bones, poorly developed feathers, and blindness — can become permanent conditions, if the animals even survive to release.

If wild creatures get used to eating human food, what will they want to eat when they're released?

Will they be able to find meat growing on trees? Where will they go to find that kind of food?

> **Cow's milk is one of the worst foods anyone can feed baby animals. It makes them sick and can kill them.**

49

FREQUENT FEATHERED FEEDERS

It would be much easier to feed baby birds if they took bottles, but how can birds suck without lips?

Besides, their parents don't give them milk. The adults drop (or stuff) insects, seeds, fruits, or meat into the babies' begging mouths or *regurgitate* (throw up) food that's been partially digested.

Rehabilitators feed each baby bird by hand at first. They use syringes or eye droppers to give the chirpers *formula* (specially prepared diet).

Photo: Karen Von den Deale

Feeding Frenzy. Volunteer Janet Teglas feeds a few of the 30-plus orphaned grackles at WILDCARE. Every spring and summer, volunteers care for hundreds of baby birds.

Photo: Critter Alley

Nestlings. Baby birds need to be fed every 20-30 minutes, dawn to dusk.

When the babies grow bigger, rehabbers use toothpicks, forceps, or fingers to feed them the kinds of foods they'll eat in the wild. These include worms, seeds, fish, berries, or chunks of meat, depending on the species.

Wild bird parents — and rehabilitators — are kept hopping from dawn until dusk, feeding nestlings as well as fledglings. Every 15 to 30 minutes, babies have to be fed and nests cleaned up.

Imagine a room full of berry baskets wriggling with tiny, naked birds, their *gaping* (wide-open) beaks shrieking, cheeping, and peeping for food. As soon as a volunteer feeds one row of begging babies, it's time to start all over again.

No wonder rehabilitators are thankful that most birds sleep at night!

MAMMAL MEALS

A baby mammal needs formula just like its mother's milk. But finding a substitute for mother's milk isn't easy. (And, no, cow's milk isn't the answer and neither is human infant formula — both cause serious problems.)

For many years, rehabilitators whipped up their own recipes. Now a few companies make and sell different baby animal formulas.

Most young mammals need to eat every few hours, day and night. Some, like raccoons and squirrels, will take formula from a bottle, eye dropper, or syringe.

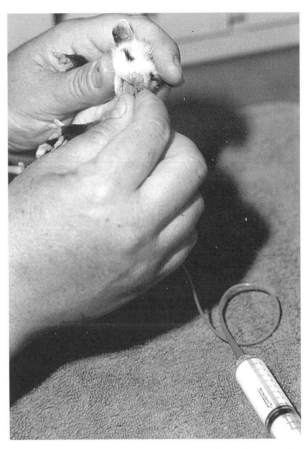

Photo: Critter Alley

Tube Feedings. *Sometimes, baby opossums need to be tube-fed.*

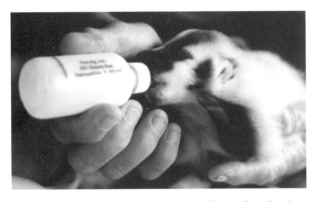

Photo: Tom Sanders

Feisty Mammals. *Even baby badgers need mother's milk or the next best thing — formula.*

But others, such as baby opossums and seriously injured animals, might have to be *tube-fed* if they can't suck.

Rehabbers do this by carefully passing a narrow tube down the animal's mouth into its stomach. Formula is slowly dribbled through the tube.

A Brave Plunge for Whales

Even sick marine mammals may need to be tube-fed. But who has the courage to tube a whale?

Becky Barron does. As director of Wildlife Rescue of Key West in Florida, Becky has helped rescue and rehabilitate several whales and dolphins.

With great trust, Becky sticks her hand (and arm) down the whales' throats, passing a tube the size of a garden hose into their stomachs. Then she pours in fresh, blenderized fish.

Needles and Pills

If animals won't eat at all, fluids and medicines can be given through a needle *intravenously* (in the vein) or *subcutaneously* (under the skin).

Wild animals don't like taking pills any more than kids do. That's why rehabilitators often crush medicines and hide them in yummy foods.

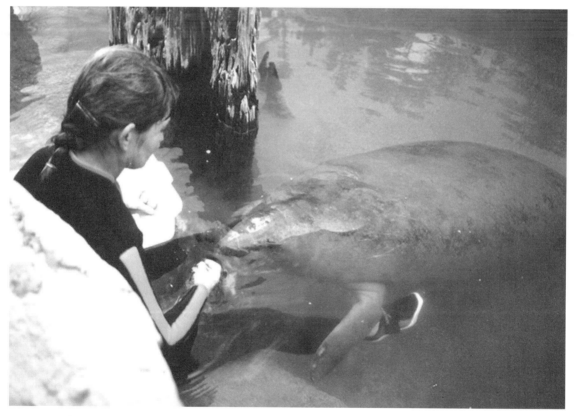

Photo: Bill Munoz

Tricky Treats. *Deborah Halin, Lowry Park Zoo's assistant curator of Florida mammals, feeds high protein pellets to a recovering manatee. Vitamins are hidden inside the tasty treats.*

Chapter 7

Bushels of Wild Babies

WILD AND CRAZY SPRINGS

Why is spring the wildest, craziest time of the year for wildlife rehabilitators? Because it's "baby season," when most wild animals give birth.

Spring is also when people pick up thousands of wild babies, assuming the little critters have been abandoned. These well-meaning people take the babies to rehabilitators, who must then fill in for mom and dad.

Photo: Lynne McCoy

No Spring Break. *Babies need to be cared for, whether they're real orphans or not.*

The work never stops — feeding dozens of babies, cleaning them up and keeping them warm, then teaching them to hunt, find food, groom themselves, fly, swim, hide, and avoid humans.

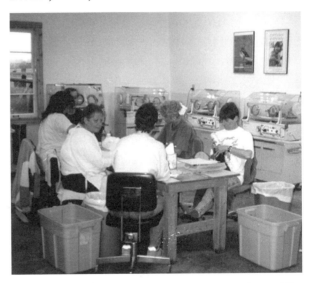

Photo: Critter Alley

Substitute Moms. *Volunteers feed orphaned babies spring and summer. Incubators in the background keep babies warm.*

Some babies taken from their mothers don't survive. That's why rehabilitators educate people about when to help (and *not* help) suspected orphans.

53

> **A baby animal's best chance for survival — always — is its mother.**

IMPRINTING

Baby animals learn very early to identify with (think they're the same species as) their mothers. This is called *imprinting*, and it helps young animals survive.

When humans raise young wild birds, there's always the risk that the birds will imprint on them instead of their own species. Then the birds may grow up thinking that they, too, are human.

Human-imprinted birds sometimes don't want to hang around or mate with their own species. If released, they often seek out people and become a nuisance or a danger. For this reason, many birds (especially raptors) that have imprinted on humans cannot be returned to the wild.

Human-loving Hawk

One example of this is Acoma, a red-tailed hawk that landed on a man's shoulder while the man was cooking chicken in his back yard. The frightened man wisely reported this to Liberty Wildlife Rehabilitation Foundation in Scottsdale, Arizona.

Like other too-friendly raptors, Acoma is human-imprinted. He was stolen from his nest and raised in someone's home.

Because he wasn't fed the kind of food a hawk needs to grow strong bones and straight wings, Acoma became weak and sick.

Photo: George Jackson

Acoma. *Because he's imprinted on people, Acoma can never be released back to the wild.*

Later, either the hawk escaped or his caretaker carelessly released him. Acoma immediately scouted out his favorite species — humans.

Because his attraction to people is unsafe, Acoma now lives permanently at Liberty Wildlife. He helps other birds by teaching people about the tragedy of stealing wildlife from the wild.

PREVENTING HUMAN-IMPRINTING

Rehabbers work hard to prevent wild animals from becoming tame or imprinting on humans. If possible, they raise babies of the same species together so they'll bond to each other instead of to humans.

When they have only one baby and can't transfer it to another center with more of that species, rehabilitators have to become very creative.

To prevent a young animal from getting used to human voices, for example, a rehabber might not talk out loud to the animal. Instead, she would play tapes of animal sounds, especially those of the baby's species. Mirrors might be put in a cage so the baby can see its own reflection.

Surrogate Mothers

Centers also might use *surrogate* (substitute) mothers such as stuffed animals or hand puppets to help feed and raise babies. As long as the human caretaker is not seen, the young animal won't get too used to people.

© 1997 The Marine Mammal Center / Photo: Ken Bach

Substitute Mom. *An orphaned sea lion nuzzles his stuffed walrus mother, who comes complete with bottles.*

When rehabilitators at Wildlife Education and Rehabilitation Center (W.E.R.C.) in Morgan Hill, California, admitted Bobbie, an orphaned bobcat kitten, they weren't sure what to do.

Photo: W.E.R.C.

Bobbie. *How could rehabilitators keep an orphaned bobcat wild and teach her survival skills?*

They knew that other rehabilitators had prevented baby birds of prey from imprinting on them by using feathered gloves or hand puppets to care for the babies.

But mammals aren't fooled so easily. They have a good sense of smell — (most birds don't). If the bobcat kitten smelled the humans who fed her, she would grow up associating human scent with food.

Learning to trust humans would be Bobbie's death sentence, because she'd probably seek out people. Unfortunately, a lot of people fear or hate bobcats and shoot them on sight.

So W.E.R.C. rehabilitators came up with a great solution. They made a fake fur bobcat costume, complete with mask.

Every day, a volunteer became Bobbie's "mother" and dressed in the costume, brushing herself with sage and bay leaves, to cover up her human smell.

Photo: W.E.R.C.

Bobbie's "Mom." *Every day a volunteer dressed in a bobcat costume, covered her smell with herbs, and taught Bobbie how to be a wild bobcat.*

Bobbie, the first bobcat raised by a surrogate mother, successfully learned to hunt and avoid people. Later, she was ear-tagged and released in the state park where she'd been found.

Bobbie has been spotted twice by park rangers. They report that she's healthy and very wild.

FOSTER PARENTS

Using *foster parents* is another way to prevent human imprinting. These are adult animals who care for babies. They often are the same species. Usually, the adults are nonreleasable because of permanent injuries or because they're human-imprinted.

Fooling the Fosters

Workers at Shelby Steel, a steel fabricating plant, called Anne Miller (Alabama Wildlife Rehabilitation Center in Birmingham) to report that barn owls had nested in the ceiling insulation. The insulation had torn apart, and the nestling owls had died after falling from the nest.

Anne had just admitted four orphaned barn owls about the same age to the rehabilitation center. She was worried about the expense of feeding them fourteen rats a day, which would cost $10.50.

Photo: Helen Connor

Barn Owl Orphans. *Feeding these babies fourteen rats a day would cost $315 a month!*

56

Anne knew the wild barn owl parents could catch plenty of rats and mice. But would they keep hunting rodents for barn owl nestlings from the wildlife center, placed in a nearby substitute nest? It was worth a try.

New Nest Box

Anne persuaded the manager of the building to let her put up a nest box, before the adult owls — who were roosting in another building — returned to find their babies gone.

The manager agreed, and company workers installed the nest box 50 feet in the air, close to the original nesting site.

Just before dusk, Anne put the four orphaned babies from the rehabilitation center into the nest box. Then she sat up all night, watching.

Photo: Greg Crenshaw

Nest Box. *Shelby Steel plant workers installed a new nest box for the owls.*

Busy, Bewildered Adults

For awhile the adults flew around, upset and bewildered because they couldn't find their nestlings," Anne said.

"Then they heard the babies in the nest box calling for food. The male flew away, obviously nervous, but the female couldn't stand it. She flew out, nabbed a mouse, and fed the babies. Then she hunted more rodents."

Photo: John Findlay III

Expert Mousers. *Barn owls catch a dozen or more rodents a day to feed their young.*

The following evening, Anne returned, using her car as a *blind* (hiding place) so the owls couldn't see her.

"By 11 o'clock, the parents had brought so much stuff I knew the babies were okay," she said.

Anne had used owl foster parents before to raise babies at the wildlife center, but this was the first time she'd combined foster parents with substitute babies, a substitute nest, and a substitute location!

Thanks to the caring cooperation of the Shelby Steel plant people and Anne's willingness to lose a lot of sleep, the four fluffy owlets found a good home.

SOCIALIZED ANIMALS

Even adult animals can become *socialized* (used to people) when they are cared for and handled. Then they lose their fear of humans.

Fear of humans protects wild animals. Without it, they cannot safely survive in the wild. Do you think it would be dangerous to release socialized or human-imprinted wild animals?

Imagine this: You are on a picnic in the mountains. Suddenly you see a black bear waddle toward you.

He's completely unafraid. Someone has raised him from a cub, and he's used to people. They give him food all the time, but you don't know that.

All you see is a huge, wild bear coming toward you. Would you appreciate his friendliness, or would you scream, run, and grab the nearest weapon?

Are people safe around this bear?

Is the bear safe around people?

What do you think will happen to this friendly bear?

Photo: Shannon K. Jacobs

Too friendly. Any wild animal that has lost its fear of humans is dangerous ... and doomed.

Chapter 8

Kids Want to Know

Q: Some boys in my school shoot birds for target practice. They said birds don't feel pain. Is that true?

A: All creatures feel pain. The difference with wild animals is that they don't show it. In the wild, any injury, sickness, or disability draws attention to an animal.

Predators are always looking for an easy meal. So the wounded suffer in silence. But they still suffer.

Photo: Critter Alley

Suffering in Silence. *Injured by a blow dart, this pigeon doesn't appear to feel pain, but it does.*

You might discuss this problem with your state wildlife agency or a wildlife rehabilitator. The boys may not know it's against the law to harm, capture, or keep wild birds.

Q: I want to bring a nest of wild bunnies to school. What should I feed them?

A: If you remove baby bunnies from their nest, they'll probably die. Rabbits are very terrified of people. They'll do anything to get away from us — even break their backs smacking into cages, trying to hop away. Stress easily kills young bunnies kept by people. Even rehabilitators have difficulty raising them.

What if all your classmates stole bunnies from their nests? Think how many bunnies would die.

Maybe you can set a good example by leaving the nest alone and telling others why they should do the same.

Why not learn about bunnies and share their fascinating natural history with your classmates? Become a bunny expert, not a bunny-napper.

Q: Are there places where kids can volunteer directly with animals?

A: There are wonderful volunteer opportunities in some rehabilitation centers. A lot depends on what kind of animals are being treated.

Marine mammals usually are too big and unpredictable for young people to work with. On the other hand, some birds might be fine. If you're interested, contact rehabilitators in your area.

Photo: Critter Alley

Young Volunteers. *Jocelyn Cutler (left) and Jennifer Sovey (right), both 14, feed fledglings at Critter Alley Wildlife Rehabilitation Center in Michigan before the birds are released.*

Photo: Caroline Brawner

Blubbery Giant. *Marine mammal centers usually don't allow young people to volunteer directly with the animals because of the creatures' size. There are many other ways to help, though.*

Q: I want to work directly with wildlife when I grow up. What careers should I plan for?

A: People usually think of veterinarians when they consider wildlife careers, but there are other choices.

Quite a few wildlife rehabilitators are *veterinary technicians* (vet techs). Vet techs are like animal care nurses. They often work in veterinary clinics, assisting veterinarians.

To become a veterinary technician, a person typically attends two or three years of school at a junior college or training institute. Then he or she must pass a certification test in order to be licensed.

Why do so many vet techs become rehabilitators? A few admit that they want more challenges than working only in clinics. They believe that wildlife medicine is an exciting new frontier.

Photo: Coleen Doucette

Vet Tech. *Coleen Doucette, a wildlife rehabilitator, gives an education program with Beth, a broad-winged hawk. Coleen feels her technical education has helped her work with wildlife, and rehabilitation experience benefits her job as a vet tech in a veterinarian clinic.*

Q: My friends and I took 12 baby ducks home to raise. Now 10 of them are dead. Will we get in trouble if we take the two living ducks to a rehabilitator?

A: Ask an adult to call a wildlife rehabilitator or your state wildlife agency right away. The best chance for the ducklings is with a rehabilitator.

It's wonderful that you want to be close to wild creatures, but you don't need to take them home to enjoy them.

Watch them in their wild world, where they will have a good chance to survive.

You won't get in trouble if you take the babies to a rehabilitator.

But, please, learn from this sad mistake — don't kidnap any more baby ducks. They need their mother's care.

Mother ducks keep their babies warm and teach them important survival skills. Most humans don't know how to do that.

Other professionals who may work directly or indirectly with wildlife are those who specialize in *biology* (all life forms), *ecology* (relationships among plants, animals, and their habitats), *zoology* (biology of animals), *herpetology* (reptiles and amphibians), and *ornithology* (birds).

It's good to get as much volunteer experience as possible. This can include working at zoos, rehabilitation centers, nature centers, veterinary clinics, or wildlife parks.

Also, check with organizations such as the Audubon Society or Sierra Club. They often offer field trips and other outdoor activities.

Q: I like the names rehabbers give to animals. Does everyone do that?

A: A few rehabbers don't. They worry they'll become too attached to the animals and have a hard time releasing them.

Others name only education animals. Some give names to all the critters, and what amazing imaginations they have!

The animals don't know their names, though. Rehabbers use names to keep track of the many animals they care for.

Susan Ahalt (Ironside Bird Rescue in Cody, Wyoming) even names *groups* of birds!

Photo: Susan Ahalt

"The Fabulous Five." *Susan rehabilitated these orphaned kestrels after their nest tree was cut down. "Dent," the youngest (with taped wing), was released a few weeks after his siblings.*

Photo: Bob Silva

"The Dream Team." *Susan raised these five house wrens (as well as four barn swallows) and released them all back to the wild.*

These are some other nifty names, from Cec and Tom Sanders (Wet MountainWildlife Rehabilitation Center in Florence, Colorado).

They love to play around with words while feeding deer in the "*doe*mitory" at the "or*fawn*age."

Photo: Tom Sanders

KimBEARly.

Photo: Tom Sanders

Quillma.

Photo: Tom Sanders

Dantelope and Diantelope.

Release – The Last Step

Photo: B.D. Wehrfritz

Healed and Free. Susan Ahalt (Ironside Bird Rescue in Cody, Wyoming) releases Piney Mack, a golden eagle she rehabilitated. With her are Dr. Bob Beiermann and his son, Clint.

Chapter 9

Setting Wildlife Free

HABITAT NEEDED

Wildlife can't be turned loose just anywhere. The site has to be good for the animals and acceptable to nearby people.

Rehabbers start searching for release sites long before the animals are freed. But it's not easy to find good habitat with abundant food, water, shelter, and little contact with humans. Unfortunately, many habitats have been disrupted or destroyed by development.

Coleen Doucette (Acadia Wildlife Foundation in Mount Desert, Maine) lives on the border of Acadia National Park. It's an ideal place for releases.

"I'm lucky because I live up here in a corner of the country where we still have some wilderness left," Coleen said. "I have about 200 acres of national park in my back yard, so I can open cage doors and let wildlife go."

Help for Habitat

At Big Sky Wildcare, a raptor rehabilitation center in Bozeman, Montana, volunteers started a Habitat Enhancement Program to create habitat for birds of prey and other wildlife.

Volunteer experts in land, bird, water, and habitat-related fields advise interested local landowners on how to manage their land to help wildlife.

Photo: Coleen Doucette

Rare Room to Run. *A fox is released in Coleen Doucette's back yard, which is Acadia National Park. Good habitat is hard to find.*

The land can range from a backyard to a big ranch. If programs like this are successful, they will ensure that eagles and other raptors have quality habitat when they're released. Without it, where will the birds go?

Photo: Bobbi Geise

Where Will Healed Eagles Go? *A Big Sky Wildcare volunteer releases a young bald eagle that was treated for poisoning. Without good habitat, recovered birds have no place to go.*

THE RELEASE PROCESS

The release process starts when animals are moved to outdoor enclosures to live with others of their own species. They get used to weather conditions and receive less and less human attention.

Enclosures may be located near forests or other habitats where the animals will be released. Some creatures even get visits from their future wild neighbors.

Before release, rehabilitators make sure the animals can fly, run, or climb normally.

They also evaluate each animal's ability to see, hear, hunt or find natural foods, relate to its own species, and avoid enemies.

Slow and Fast Releases

In a slow release, the door of the pen or carrier is left open so the animal can come and go as it wants. The animal may be placed on a branch or other safe place, away from predators.

Food is kept at the release site until the rehabber knows that the animal is hunting or finding its own food. Slow releases are helpful for orphans.

Photo: Critter Alley

Slow Release. *These young raccoons will receive food until they are able to survive on their own.*

In a fast release, the animal is taken to a release site and let go. Ideally, that is close to where the animal was found.

Fast releases are good for wilder creatures who don't need (or want) anything to do with people. This is especially true for animals admitted as adults.

Sea Lion Release. *Ken Lee (center) and other TMMC volunteers release rehabilitated sea lions on a beach.*

THE HARD CHOICE RELEASE

When a wild animal's injuries are too serious for recovery, the rehabilitator has to ask hard questions. Should the animal have to suffer in pain or forced captivity, or should it be *euthanized* (quickly, painlessly killed)?

The decision is never easy, and rehabilitators agonize over the decision. But most would rather euthanize an animal than return it to the wild if it can't survive on its own. In the wild it would suffer by slow starvation, or it would be hurt or killed by predators.

Tribute to Twilight

One unfortunate example of this was Twilight, a young red-tailed hawk that had been kept illegally. Neglected by his captor, Twilight suffered from blindness and other health problems caused by poor diet and improper care.

Twilight was rescued and taken to Lynne McCoy, an independent rehabilitator in East Tennessee. Lynne paid special attention to the gentle bird, trying to make up for his losses.

When Twilight developed an infection in his head, Lynne took him to her veterinarian. An x-ray showed a lead pellet lodged in his brain where the hawk had been shot.

Photo: Lynne McCoy

Twilight. *A gentle, trusting bird.*

The infection got worse. When antibiotics and tender, loving care couldn't help anymore, Lynne gave Twilight the last kindness she could offer — euthanasia.

Later, weeping as she penned a tribute to Twilight in her newsletter, Lynne wrote, "In my heart a red-tail is soaring high, eyes bright, free of pain. Good-bye, Twilight."

Trapping Torment

The sheriff's department called Janet Walker (Critter Alley Wildlife Rehabilitation Center in Grand Ledge, Michigan) to report a raccoon limping along a highway. A steel-jawed leghold trap was clamped to her paw.

When Janet found her, the raccoon was curled up in shock; the trap had nearly cut off her paw. A nursing mother, she had tried to chew off the rest of her paw to get back to her babies.

Janet knew the raccoon's mangled paw would have to be amputated. She also knew that the front paws on a raccoon are very important for their survival. They use them for finding food in water, prying open shellfish, feeding, walking, running, and climbing.

With a heavy heart, Janet decided to euthanize the raccoon rather than send her into a hopeless future. When the babies couldn't be found, Janet's heartache was doubled. She knew they would die of starvation without their mother.

Photo: Critter Alley

70

Chapter 10

Kids Want to Know

Q: Do rehabilitators ever get bitten or scratched by the animals they treat?

A: Most rehabilitators probably would admit to being bitten, scratched, or jabbed a few times. After all, helpless animals have to defend themselves the best way they can — with teeth, claws, and beaks.

A part of training to become a rehabilitator involves learning how to properly handle wild critters. This skill protects the animals and people.

Photo: Shannon K. Jacobs

Don't Badger Me! *Learning how to safely handle all kinds of critters is an important part of wildlife rehabilitation.*

Q: Why do rehabilitators euthanize animals? Aren't they supposed to save, not kill them?

A: The goal of rehabilitation is to help sick, orphaned or injured wildlife *recover and return to the wild*. Unfortunately, not all animals recover.

About half of the animals admitted to rehabilitation centers can't be released. They're either too badly injured or too seriously sick. Some of these creatures live in constant pain. Others have lost their eyesight, legs, wings, or beaks. They can't eat, fly, or walk.

Should these animals be confined to cages, forever yearning to be free? Do they have a right to be released from pain and suffering? In the wild, they would go hungry, or predators (including people) would hurt or kill them.

Permit requirements don't allow rehabilitators to keep unreleasable animals unless they are education animals (which require other, special permits). Even if they could keep them, how could rehabilitators pay for the care of hundreds of thousands of hopelessly sick or injured wild animals?

With so little money available to treat wildlife, wouldn't that money be better spent on animals that are able to survive in the wild?

Choosing to euthanize an animal is a very painful decision. Some rehabbers cry their eyes out, and it never gets easier for them. The only thing that helps is knowing that they've released the animal from a life of misery.

What about the people who harmed the animals in the first place — what responsibility do they have in the suffering and death of wildlife?

What can we all do to prevent wildlife injuries so these painful decisions don't have to be made?

Q: How many rehabilitated animals are released?

A: Generally, less than half. That may not sound very high, but remember that many of these animals are severely injured or dangerously sick when admitted.

What happens to the animals that aren't released? Most of them die or are euthanized. A few are kept as permanent education animals or transferred to other centers, museums, or zoos for displays or for *captive breeding* (breeding wild animals in captivity to produce young).

Q: How can people help rehabilitators?

1. Donate money. Rehabilitators always need help with expenses.

2. Ask rehabilitators if they have a "wish list." These are items they always need, from animal foods and paper towels to computers and vehicles.

3. Become a volunteer. You may be needed to build or clean cages, feed and rescue animals, answer phones, or help with fundraising.

Photo: Critter Alley

Wildlife Hero. *For two and a half years, 13-year-old Mark July has spent his Sundays volunteering at Critter Alley Wildlife Rehabilitation Center in Michigan.*

4. Join a local wildlife rehabilitation organization. Basic memberships vary from $10 to $25 a year. Usually you'll get at least one newsletter published by the center. These feature rescue tips, information about various animals, and stories about the critters cared for at the center.

You, your family, or your classroom can "adopt" an animal if you donate money at a certain level to help pay for its care. A photo of the animal may be sent to you, or you may get to name it.

Some centers let adoptive parents help with the animal's release. If it's an education animal, your class might receive a visit.

5. Ask for a really wild birthday present. Send family and friends the name and address of your favorite wildlife rehabilitation center. Ask them to make a donation, take out a membership, or sponsor an adoption in your name. It's a great gift for everyone!

6. Tell others about rehabilitators.

7. Learn how to prevent wildlife injuries (see Chapter 17).

8. Don't be a baby-napper (see Chapters 3 and 17).

Photo: Shannon K. Jacobs

Adopted Bird Visit. *Jacki Wallace, a volunteer with Birds of Prey Foundation, holds Chaco, an education bird (Swainson's hawk). Chaco was adopted by this sixth-grade class.*

Learning More About Wildlife

Photo: Rosemary Perfit

Ready for School. *Susan Ahalt (Ironside Bird Rescue in Cody, Wyoming) and Snap, a great horned education owl, pause before giving a school presentation.*

Chapter 11

Sharing the Wonder

EXCITING SCHOOL PROGRAMS

Teaching people about wildlife is very important to rehabilitators. They answer countless questions over the phone, teach anyone who brings them an animal, and give thousands of structured education programs a year.

All these methods of education help children and adults learn about wildlife habitats and *native* animals (those that live naturally in certain areas), endangered species, peaceful ways to live with wildlife, and ways to protect wild creatures.

Bat Woman

When Penny Murphy (Urban Wildlife Rescue in Aurora, Colorado) visits schools, she shows fantastic slides of bats.

She also passes around a few stuffed bats. They were alive once, but after they died from their injuries, Penny had them stuffed so kids could touch them.

During Penny's programs, students learn about the importance of bats, ways to protect them, and why they should never touch bats on the ground.

Even kids who enter the room afraid of bats soon become batty for the furry, flying mammals.

Photo: Shannon K. Jacobs

Safe School Bats. *Penny Murphy takes stuffed bats to schools during her education programs, so kids can touch them safely. (Notice the bat sticker on her cheek?)*

Nonreleasable Animals

Some rehabilitators hold educational permits. These allow them to keep nonreleasable wild animals and use them in education programs. (These permits don't allow animals being rehabilitated for release to be used for education.)

Which animals are considered nonreleasable? Those that have permanent injuries that prevent them from surviving in the wild.

Photo: Lynne McCoy

Squirrely Teacher. *Megan, a squirrel blinded by pesticide spray, visited many classrooms in East Tennessee with rehabilitator Lynne McCoy.*

For example, some birds can survive with only one eye or one leg. But if part of a wing is missing, they won't be able to fly or hunt. Many birds that are human-imprinted cannot be released.

Animal Teachers

Education animals are great teachers. It's quite an honor to get a visit from an eagle, turtle, snake, or opossum.

Just because an animal can't be released doesn't mean it likes to be around people. Education animals have to be trained to tolerate noisy crowds. Some never learn to accept humans and cannot be used in education programs.

Diane Johnson (Operation Wildlife in Linwood, Kansas) visits a lot of schools, taking education raptors with her. Before she takes the birds into a public setting, she trains them several hours a day for six to twelve months.

How does Diane train raptors to put up with people? She described it as a "long process with a lot of repetition."

At night, after her three children are asleep, Diane grabs a book and sits down next to a new eagle or hawk in its cage. She reads aloud for a few hours at a time, letting the bird get used to her voice.

When the bird has learned to tolerate her, Diane slowly begins to introduce it to other people.

Photo: KDWP

Fairy Tale Tonight? *Diane Johnson reads aloud to new education animals, such as this bald eagle, to allow them to adjust to people slowly.*

78

Summer Vacations - for the Birds?

At Liberty Wildlife Rehabilitation Foundation in Scottsdale, Arizona, 30 raptors are kept as education birds. *Manning* (training) the new education birds is a slow and respectful process, according to volunteer educator Anne Steinmetz.

Each day, the birds are fed (some by hand) in the same place at the same time, so they know what to expect from their human caretakers.

The birds slowly get used to wearing *jesses* (leather leg straps). Jesses allow trainers to catch the birds without having to grab bodies or wings and possibly injure the birds. The trainers can then teach the birds to step up and stand on a glove. When the birds are comfortable on a glove, they begin meeting other people.

From October through May, the education birds at Liberty Wildlife travel to many schools and community centers around the Phoenix area. They teach people the rapture of raptors.

In June, off come those jesses. Like other hard-working teachers, Liberty Wildlife birds earn their summers off!

ARRANGING EDUCATION VISITS

If your class would like a visit from a rehabilitator with education animals, ask your teacher to get a list of nearby wildlife rehabilitators with education permits. The teacher can call your state wildlife agency for information.

If you're fortunate enough to see a school or community program with live education animals, your class might want to discuss how to act quietly and respectfully in the animal's presence.

Photo: Shannon K. Jacobs

Respectful Group. *Preschoolers listen to Birds of Prey Foundation volunteer Jacki Wallace talk about Spud, a screech owl education bird.*

TOURING REHAB CENTERS

Some centers, especially large ones, will let individuals or schools tour part of the facilities. Others may not have enough room to separate sick animals from crowds of people, so they don't allow visits.

Since the main purpose is to care for wildlife, each rehabilitator has to weigh the advantages of letting people visit the center.

Even if your group is able to tour a center, you probably won't get to see all the animals. Those that are being rehabilitated for release cannot be seen by the public. It's very important that visitors respect this. The animals get very stressed around humans, and they need to stay as wild as possible, so they'll survive when released.

A few centers have one-way glass in front of enclosures, so visitors can watch the animals without being seen.

This would be an ideal way for the public to experience the incredible work of rehabilitators. Unfortunately, it's very expensive, and most centers can't afford it.

Photo: Jonathan X. Di Cesare

'Possum in the Park. Denise Hill-Hollyday (holding an opossum education animal) fascinates her young audience with a wildlife program at Burroughs Park in Tomball, Texas. Denise is an educator with Friends of Texas Wildlife, a nonprofit support group for Wildlife Center of Harris County Precinct 4.

Chapter 12

Is There a Skunk in Your House?

HANDLING WILDLIFE CONFLICTS

If there are bats in your attic or raccoons in the chimney, your family might consider calling a wildlife rehabilitator to learn how to evict the animals without killing or harming them.

Photo: Urban Wildlife Rescue

High Anxiety. *Penny Murphy shows a tree company worker how to rescue a family of raccoons living in a tree that will be cut down.*

"Pest" or animal control companies, on the other hand, often poison or trap (and kill) wild animals living in and around people's homes.

Rehabilitators also suggest effective ways to prevent animals from entering your home in the first place. This is a very important step to take, or more furred tenants will move in fast.

Designer Bat Houses

A good example of the difference rehabilitators can make in a community is in Mineral Wells, Texas. That's where Amanda Lollar, director of Bat World Sanctuary and Educational Center, lives.

Amanda is a bat rehabilitator and an expert on Mexican free-tails (Texas' most common bat). She has designed bat houses specifically for these little critters.

Amanda also taught local people how to put up the bat houses as alternate roosting sites. That way, when people evict the bats from vacant buildings and attics, the animals have somewhere to go.

Like most wild animals, bats are losing their habitat. Often, the only shelters available to them are human structures.

In the past, people usually killed bats that roosted inside homes and buildings. That was a bad solution for everyone.

But Mineral Wells citizens know how to evict bat colonies *and* keep their bug-eating benefits. (One tiny bat can eat 500 mosquitoes an hour!)

Citizens have mounted more than 40 new bat houses in the town. These colorful (and, sometimes, humorous) houses provide habitat for thousands of Mexican free-tailed bats that desperately need homes.

Photo: Amanda Lollar

Bat House Humor. *A home for evicted bats, mounted on the side of a hair salon, is one of many bat houses in Mineral Wells, Texas.*

TELEPHONE ADVICE

Most rehabilitators give wildlife advice over the phone. They answer questions about wildlife behavior, offer options when human-wildlife conflicts occur, and refer callers to agencies that can help them.

Photo: Critter Alley

Juggling Duties. *Sue Philp answers calls at Critter Alley Wildlife Rehabilitation Center in Michigan. A box of orphaned raccoons waits to be admitted.*

People sometimes call rehabilitators to report problems with wildlife, animals that are injured or orphaned, or incidents of abuse, neglect, or harassment of wildlife.

In one case, a person called Alabama Wildlife Rescue Service hotline to report a neighbor who was using a raccoon as live bait to train his hunting dogs.

Knowing it was against Alabama state law to keep a raccoon without a permit, the hotline volunteer told staff members about the incident. The staff contacted a game warden, who confiscated the raccoon.

He took the animal to the rehabilitation center for treatment. It was released later. But the man who kept the raccoon was prosecuted for illegal possession and abuse of a wild animal.

Volunteers all over the country give phone advice, handling hundreds of calls a year, saving people (and governments) money and preventing unnecessary suffering for animals.

HUMANE SOLUTIONS

When a landlord discovered a family of raccoons living in the attic of his apartment building, he called Jack Murphy at Urban Wildlife Rescue in Aurora, Colorado.

The renters and the landlord wanted the raccoons out of there, but they didn't want them hurt.

The landlord was lucky to find Jack Murphy and his wife, Penny. They are experts at using humane solutions to solve wildlife conflicts.

In a typical year, the Murphys handle more than 3,000 hotline calls, saving at least 8,000 animals. (That's in addition to the 200-plus injured and orphaned creatures they rehabilitate at their home-based center.)

Jack explained to the landlord that raccoons (just like squirrels) usually have at least two dens. The solution, then, was to make the mother feel unwelcome in the building. Maybe then, she'd get the hint, pack up the babies, and move to another den.

The landlord put a bright light in the attic and made a lot of noise, as Jack suggested. But Momma Raccoon wouldn't budge. She was no fool. It was snowing outside, and the attic was warm and cozy.

The landlord refused to harm the animals or dump them out in the cold. Instead, he made a pest of himself, increasing the noise and light levels in the attic. Finally, the weary raccoon mother packed up her babies and moved out one night.

Everyone benefited from the patience and kindness of the landlord. The raccoon family stayed together, and many people learned about safe and caring choices when dealing with unwanted, furry guests.

Photo: Urban Wildlife Rescue

Supporting Wildlife. *Penny Murphy operates a booth at Wild Oats Market, which was donating a portion of the day's sale to Urban Wildlife Rescue (UWR). Penny answered many questions about UWR's services, which include advising people how to humanely evict wild critters from their homes.*

Trashing Babies

Another person wasn't nearly as kind. When this homeowner found raccoons living in his chimney, he chased off the mother and dumped the six babies in a trash can. For two days, the baby raccoons sweltered inside the metal can.

Someone heard about the heartless act and called Penny. The starving, frightened babies were rescued.

If the homeowner had tried a humane solution, the mother raccoon would have moved her babies out. Instead, Penny and Jack became foster parents for the six orphaned raccoons.

It was a lot of work and expense for the Murphys. They had many other baby animals to care for.

The raccoon kits were lucky, though. With the nurturing care they received at Urban Wildlife Rescue, the masked bandits grew into healthy wild animals. As soon as the raccoons were old enough to survive on their own, they were released.

Photo: Urban Wildlife Rescue

Saved From the Dump. *If the homeowner who found this raccoon family had called a rehabilitator, he would have learned how to humanely evict the family, and the babies could have stayed with their mother.*

Chapter 13

Improving Wildlife Treatment

RESEARCH

In order to manage wildlife properly, scientists and biologists need to learn as much as possible about them. But it's hard to study animals in the wild.

Rehabilitation centers provide excellent opportunities to investigate wild creatures in temporary captivity.

In some centers, scientists are researching treatments for wildlife diseases, lead poisoning, and oil-soaked animals. Other research focuses on learning more about specific animals or endangered species.

Bat Courtship

As the only volunteer rehabilitator at Bat World Sanctuary (Mineral Wells, Texas), Amanda Lollar has spent about 15,000 hours with a colony of 50 Mexican free-tailed bats.

She has observed them closely while handfeeding them. The bats are used to Amanda, so they act naturally.

This has allowed her to witness courting and mating behavior that's never been seen before with free-tails.

Amanda also has recorded free-tail courting songs. These sounds may help biologists identify key caves in the wild where free-tails breed.

If the caves can be protected, it will be an important step in saving Mexican free-tails. Their numbers are declining at an alarming rate.

Photo: Amanda Lollar

Mexican Free-tailed Bat. *Amanda Lollar's observations of a captive colony of free-tails may help save the species, which is declining in the wild.*

What Do Manatees Hear?

A researcher at the Manatee Hospital (Lowry Park Zoo in Tampa, Florida) is studying the hearing of manatees. Can they hear motorboats coming toward them in enough time to get away?

New information has been discovered about manatees' hearing. The bad news is that they can't hear motorboats, because their hearing frequency is different from humans.

The good news is that we now know what manatees can hear. With this information, new research can center on developing manatee warning devices within the animals' hearing range.

Since endangered manatees are regularly injured and killed by speed boats, this kind of research will help protect these gentle mammals.

POST-RELEASE STUDIES

Many centers do *post-release* (after release) studies to find out what happens to rehabilitated animals.

Radio transmitters are placed on the animals, and researchers track them, using receivers.

Post-release studies tell rehabilitators where their former patients go and how they adjust to the wild. This is particularly important when large predators such as cougars and bears are released. Wildlife officials want to be sure they stay far away from people.

Following Black Bears

Cec and Tom Sanders (Wet Mountain Wildlife Rehabilitation Center in Florence, Colorado) have cared for 33 young black bears over the past several years. Several bears they rehabilitated were radiocollared and tracked after release.

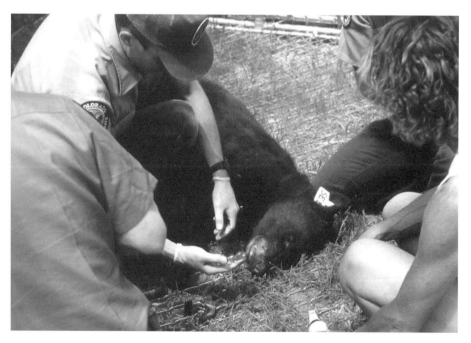

Photo: Tom Sanders

Collaring Black Bears. State wildlife officials tranquilized this rehabilitated black bear orphan and fit a radiocollar around his neck. Once released, the bear can be tracked for follow up.

"The bears did fine," Cec said. "Wildlife officials are finding that cubs seem to stay put when they're relocated. They don't try to return. Maybe that's because they don't have a territory yet."

That's very important in states like Colorado with a "two strikes and you're dead" policy for bears.

A bear that is considered a problem (has had conflicts with people) is ear-tagged and relocated to wilderness areas twice. If the bear returns or gets in trouble after that, it's killed.

Tracking Seals

For the past several years, The Marine Mammal Center in Sausalito, California, has tracked orphaned harbor seals after release. Researchers have learned a lot about how seals manage on their own.

How are seals tracked? Tiny radio transmitters are carefully glued to fur on the back of the seals' heads.

© 1997 The Marine Mammal Center / Photo: Jane Oka

Wired for Release. *Two harbor seals pups wear radio transmitters glued to their fur.*

Then researchers follow the animals' activities for three to six months. When the seals *molt* (shed their old fur), the transmitters fall off.

MEDICAL AND SURGICAL ADVANCES

Wild animals sometimes benefit from treatments for domestic animals. A dramatic example of this is Helmethead, a red-tailed hawk that made medical history in Morgan Hill, California.

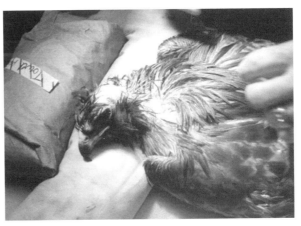

Photo: W.E.R.C.

Missing: Head Feathers. *Helmethead, an injured red-tailed hawk, waits for surgery.*

Helmethead was rescued by Sue Howell, director of Wildlife Education and Rehabilitation Center. The hawk suffered from a head injury, infected scalp, and missing head feathers.

Sue took the hawk to Dr. John Quick of the Animal Medical Clinic, who ordered medicated bandages for the restless raptor's head. No problem — Sue designed a special hat that looked like a helmet (and named the hawk after it).

87

During the next year of recovery, Helmethead's infection cleared up, and she got stronger. But she still had a serious problem — no scalp feathers.

Birds need all their feathers in perfect condition for flying and for staying warm and dry. Even missing head feathers can affect their ability to survive.

The veterinarian decided to do a sliding skin graft surgery on the bald hawk. Although this surgery had been performed before on cats and dogs, it had never been done on birds.

The procedure involved cutting some of the hawk's neck skin (with feathers), and stretching the skin over her head.

When Helmethead woke up from the surgery, she had a fringe of neck feathers on the back of her head. More feathers were expected to grow in time.

The hawk recovered well, and everyone celebrated when she was released a few months later. Helmethead was spotted a year and a half after release, still going strong.

OIL SPILLS

For many years, wildlife rehabilitators have contributed vital help during oil spills.

In 1989, they quickly responded to the Exxon Valdez oil spill in Alaska. This worst spill in U.S. history happened when a supertanker ran aground, dumping 11 million gallons of crude oil into Prince William Sound.

That day, the waters of Prince William Sound were filled with marine animals, sea birds, and flocks of migrating birds. Thousands of animals died immediately from the *toxic* (poisonous) effects of the spreading oil. Others became very sick.

Oil destroys the waterproofing and insulating properties of feathers and fur. If not treated immediately, oiled animals die from cold, starvation, pneumonia, or kidney disease.

While in such weakened conditions, they are helpless against predators. The predators also become poisoned by the oil if they eat the oiled prey.

Photo: W.E.R.C.

Getting Stronger. *A newly feathered Helmethead strengthens her wings, preparing for freedom.*

Oiled Animal Rehabilitation

Oiled animal rehabilitation is a specialized treatment that should be done by or supervised by wildlife rehabilitators who are specially trained in oiled animal care. Untrained people may not understand that oil is toxic if fumes are inhaled or if oil gets on the skin.

Experienced rehabilitators also know how to protect animals from the deadly effects of stress during capture, treatment, and release.

Most oiled animals can't eat because they're too sick. Rehabilitators tube-feed them or give them fluids and medications intravenously.

When the animals' conditions become stable, volunteers begin the long, hard job of washing oil out of fur and feathers.

Wildlife rehabilitators saved hundreds of birds and mammals in Prince William Sound. It took enormous skill, expense, and teamwork. The knowledge gained from treating so many animals at once was invaluable for the future. Every year, there are hundreds of oil spills in U.S. waters.

Some rehab centers have formed their own oil-response teams. They share their knowledge with other wildlife people, teaching them the most effective and up-to-date methods in caring for oiled animals.

Preventing Oil Spills

Most oiled animals don't survive, even with the skill and courageous efforts of many volunteers trying to save them. That is why prevention of oil spills is the most important way to avoid the tragedies of oiled wildlife.

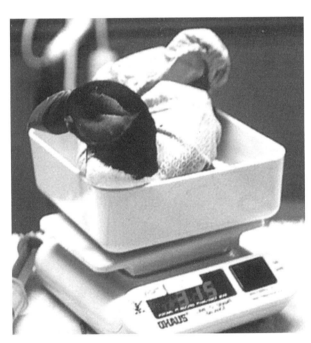

Photo: Karen Von den Deale

Oiled Bird. *An Atlantic puffin was wrapped in a bootie (operating room paper slipper) to keep the bird from preening (cleaning itself) and swallowing oil.*

Photo: Karen Von den Deale

Clean as a Whistle. *After receiving successful oiled bird treatment at WILD CARE, Inc., the puffin was released.*

Rehabilitating Mammals and Reptiles

Photo: Critter Alley

Fawn Therapy. *Janet Walker, director of Critter Alley Wildlife Rehabilitation Center in Grand Ledge, Michigan, gives physical therapy to a fawn with an injured leg.*

Chapter 14

Healers at Work

WORKING WITH LAND ANIMALS

Even in big cities, wild animals share our space. You may never see them, but all kinds of *nocturnal* (active at night) critters (raccoons, opossums, foxes, coyotes, skunks, and bats) prowl around in the dark.

Photo: Critter Alley

Night Prowler. *Skunks are nocturnal animals.*

Other creatures — snakes, squirrels, groundhogs, turtles, and bears — are more noticeable because they're *diurnal* (active in the daytime). A few, such as deer and rabbits, are *crepuscular* (mostly active at dusk and dawn).

Like birds and sea mammals, land animals are completely dependent on their habitat for survival. Humans can always move to another house, town, or state, but wild creatures rely on very specific wild foods and dwellings.

When wildlife homes are destroyed, some animals are killed instantly. Others are driven away. Rehabilitators receive some of these displaced animals, along with the huge challenge of finding decent habitat for release.

HIBERNATION

Some land animals living in cold climates *hibernate* (sleep through the winter). Hibernation helps animals, such as groundhogs, chipmunks, ground squirrels, and marmots, survive when food sources aren't available.

During hibernation, the breathing and heart rate slow down, and the body temperature drops a few degrees. These changes help to conserve energy so animals can survive the winter with little or no food.

Hibernation and Rehabilitation

How does hibernation affect rehabilitation? It can influence when an animal is released. For example, if it's October, and a groundhog is ready for release but doesn't have enough body fat to survive four to six months without eating, the animal can't be released.

Animals prepare for hibernation by wolfing down enormous amounts of food, starting in late summer. They have to put on enough body fat to last them through the winter. If injured animals are still recovering, and it's close to hibernation time, rehabbers may "winter" them at the center. This allows their healing processes to continue.

RABIES

Another consideration is the threat of rabies. In some states, rehabbers aren't allowed to work with bats, skunks, coyotes, raccoons, or foxes, because they most often get rabies and infect other animals. Some states require rehabilitators to take special training classes to learn how to safely handle rabies vector species and to prevent the spread of diseases.

Most rehabbers protect themselves by getting vaccinations against rabies. Then, if they're bit or scratched by a rabid animal, they'll need just booster shots.

REPTILES

Unlike mammals, reptiles don't maintain a steady body temperature. They rely on their surroundings to warm them up and cool them off. Because of these temperature needs, reptiles live in very specific places.

Releasing rehabilitated reptiles back to the wild must be done carefully. Some reptiles live in tiny territories. If they're removed from that territory and released somewhere else, they may not reproduce or survive.

Photo: Shannon K. Jacobs

Gila Monster. *This poisonous reptile, stolen from the wild and kept as a "pet," cannot be released because it might be carrying diseases that could wipe out a wild population.*

Sometimes, turtles that are moved from a territory being developed will return to that area when released. They end up crushed by bulldozers.

Captive reptiles pick up diseases easily. If released, they may spread the diseases to wild, endangered populations.

That's why people who are not rehabilitators should never turn animals loose into the wild. Only wildlife rehabilitators or state wildlife officials should do this.

LYNNE MCCOY

Location: Morristown, Tennessee
Description: Independent rehabilitator, treating 250 to 350 small mammals, birds, and reptiles a year
Staff: Lynne (licensed),her husband, and one part-time volunteer
Funding: Accepts donations; mostly funded by the McCoys; not a nonprofit center
Newsletter: *It's a WildLife*, published four times a year
Programs: 10-20 school and community education programs annually
Tours: No

For more than 26 years, Lynne McCoy has cared for many colorful critters with the help of her husband, David, and other volunteers. She also advises hundreds of people over the phone about wildlife issues.

Lynne works closely with Dr. Stephen Burns, a local veterinarian who enjoys using his skills to help wildlife.

Photo: Lynne McCoy

Crow Attack. *Dr. Stephen Burns examines a great horned owl that was knocked out of a tree by crows.*

Photo: David McCoy

Joy of Release. *Lynne McCoy sets free a healed red-tailed hawk, Remington. The bird had been shot in the wing.*

"What keeps me going," Lynne said, "is seeing a bird fly free, a squirrel go up a tree, or an opossum waddle off after I helped it over the bad times. I like knowing an animal is back where it belongs.

"Sometimes injured animals just need time to rest and heal," she explained. "In the wild, they don't get that. When they're helpless, they get nailed fast."

Somehow Lynne finds the time to publish a wildly entertaining newsletter, *It's a Wildlife*, four times a year. Each issue is filled with true stories, fascinating facts, and helpful hints about the wildlife Lynne helps.

Always enjoying a laugh, Lynne generously sprinkles the newsletters with her hilarious sense of humor.

Jake the Entertainer

When giving school programs, Lynne likes to take education animals with her. One animal that stole the spotlight most often was Jake, the opossum.

Photo: Lynne McCoy

Jake the Opossum. Unreleasable because of permanent injuries, Jake was an education animal that loved to show off his manners for school kids.

For many students, Jake was the first opossum they'd ever seen up close. And what an impression he made! Before each program, Jake would wrap his tail around Lynne's wrist for extra support, before meeting his loud, adoring fans.

Jake enjoyed showing off his table manners by spoon-feeding himself. He'd learned that skill while recovering from a broken jaw he'd suffered after getting hit by a car. Lynne had spoon-fed the opossum for several weeks.

In his short lifetime, Jake entertained, educated, and inspired thousands of children and hundreds of adults.

The finest tribute paid to this gentle marsupial was when a former elementary student said to Lynne, "Because of Jake, I check the pouches of all road-killed opossums, in case there are babies to save."

Jake would've been so proud. He died in his sleep, as peacefully as he had lived.

Whistler's Mother?

Whistledigger was hairless and the size of a thumb when a dog snatched her. Luckily, the dog was a retriever and knew how to carry his mouthful home tenderly, causing just minor bite wounds.

The only problem was, nobody knew what the dog had brought home!

A veterinary clinic asked if Lynne would care for the mystery animal, so she examined the critter.

Photo: Lynne McCoy

Mystery. What did the dog bring home?

She knew it was a rodent, but what kind? After ruling out what it wasn't, Lynne figured out what it was.

"Groundhog!" she announced.

Normally, groundhogs are well developed by the time they leave their burrows. So where had this baby come from?

Lynne thought Whistledigger may have been dropped by her mom or flooded out of her home.

Because she had no other groundhogs at the time, Lynne put the critter in with another orphan, a little raccoon named Sugarbear.

Sugarbear had been left behind when his mother moved all her babies except Sugarbear, who was a runt. The groundhog and raccoon played and slept together, wrestled, and fought over the water bowl.

Photo: Lynne McCoy

Temporary Roomies. *Sugarbear and Whistledigger share a room, until others of their species are admitted.*

Lynne named the groundhog Whistledigger because she whistled when she wanted attention.

Groundhogs make several sounds, including high-pitched whistles. Did that make Lynne "Whistler's Mother?" her husband David asked.

Whistledigger grew up fast. She beat her raccoon roommate to freedom. (Sugarbear was released later with other raccoons in a remote state park, far away from people.)

Summer of the Rowdy Raccoons

When they admitted four baby raccoons at one time, Lynne and David geared themselves up for a wild and crazy summer. They weren't disappointed.

The first to arrive was Rikki, the only raccoon in his family to survive when his nest tree was cut down. Rikki chittered and purred next to Bun-rab, an orphaned rabbit who became his temporary roommate.

Photo: Lynne McCoy

Rikki and Bun-rab. *Furry dreamers keep each other warm, until more orphaned raccoons arrive.*

Rachel came next. She'd been found along a highway. Lynne figured Rachel's mother had dropped the furry bundle while moving her.

Two other baby coons, Rocket and Racket, a brother and sister, were found starving in the woods. They were so young they still had their eyes closed. (Raccoon babies open their eyes about the third week of life.)

Lynne and David raised all four baby raccoons together, feeding them, keeping them warm, and laughing at their funny tricks and treats.

Photo: Lynne McCoy

A Four-Coon Night. Rikki, Rachel, Rocket, and Racket keep each other company.

When the youngsters grew into restless teenagers, Lynne took them to another rehabilitation center with a big outdoor cage. Although she knew it was time to leave the young animals, Lynne had a hard time letting them go.

She said that walking away from those young raccoons was one of the hardest things she's ever done.

Something to Think About

Rehabilitators understand why people want to keep wild babies as pets. But they also know what kind of future awaits a "tame" wild animal.

In her newsletter, Lynne described why wild ones don't make good pets:

"Gee this baby squirrel is cute, and so is the baby raccoon, and I just know they'll make wonderful pets." WRONG.

Those cute babies grow up, and cute habits aren't so cute anymore. Wrestling with the little squirrel and raccoon ... soon the squirrel bites, and those teeth are like chisels.

The little coon weighs 20 pounds, and wrestling isn't such fun anymore, but the coon doesn't know why you won't play. He's bored so he destroys the house or bites (they bite when they can't have their way) and won't accept discipline. He tears up his cage.

But he's been fed candy and is people-oriented, and now has cataracts (cloudy lens of the eyes caused from malnutrition), and the squirrel has chewed through the phone wire. Or, even worse, the raccoon has been declawed to protect the furniture.

Now you don't want them anymore ... but no zoo will accept them, no one else wants them for pets ... so you turn them loose ...and they die in miserable ways — attacks from other animals, slow starvation, or going up to strangers and acting friendly and getting shot or beaten to death.

But in reality, these animals were as good as dead the day you decided to keep them as pets.

Photo: Urban Wildlife Rescue

When Cute Babies Get Big. Don't steal babies from the wild to keep as pets. They are dangerous and unmanageable as adults, and no one wants them.

BAT WORLD SANCTUARY & EDUCATIONAL CENTER

Location:	Mineral Wells, Texas
Description:	Bat rehabilitation center and lifetime sanctuary for non-releasable bats
Staff:	One volunteer rehabilitator
Funding:	Education programs, private donations, newsletter subscriptions
Newsletter:	*Bat World News,* published quarterly
Programs:	Field trips, guided tours for school and civic groups; "Bat Chat" assemblies at North Central Texas schools
Tours:	Yes, with admission donation and by reservation; open every second Saturday and third Sunday of the month, September - May

Photo: Luanne Albright

The Enchanted Forest. *Amanda Lollar gives students a tour of the rainforest habitat she built for the 100-plus resident bats at Bat World. Visitors can see bats, such as Bucko (upper right) up close, but they can't touch them.*

In 1994, Amanda Lollar sold her furniture business and got the proper permits to start Bat World, a sanctuary and educational center for bats. It's also a permanent home for 100 nonreleasable bats.

Most of the permanent residents have been confiscated from illegal pet traders, used in research, orphaned, or permanently injured. A large colony of Mexican free-tailed bats are among them.

When schools or community groups take field trips to Bat World, visitors can walk through Amanda's miniature Enchanted Forest, where ten different species of bats in natural habitat flight cages can be seen.

.

Sunshine

Although she's dedicated to educating others about the wonder of bats, Amanda understands fears about them. She used to consider bats "vermin" too. But that was before she met Sunshine.

In 1988, Amanda found an injured Mexican free-tail bat lying on a hot downtown sidewalk. Taking pity on the poor creature, Amanda moved it into shade.

She wanted the bat to be able to die in peace. But when the bat didn't die, Amanda took it home. She then hurried to the library to read up on bats. That's when she discovered how fascinating and helpful the furry animals are.

Amanda named the Mexican free-tail Sunshine and took care of her until the little bat died two years later. In 1991, Amanda wrote *The Bat in My Pocket.* It's a beautiful book about her close relationship with Sunshine. Many people who read the book say they'll never feel the same way about bats again.

Amanda is a licensed rehabilitator who has been vaccinated against rabies. She reminds people — especially kids — to *never touch a bat.* Kids should always get an adult if they find a grounded bat. Although most bats are not diseased, no one should take a chance.

Amanda puts in long days at Bat World. Just taking care of nonreleasable bats takes six to eight hours a day. Then she rehabilitates orphaned, sick, and injured bats in a separate room.

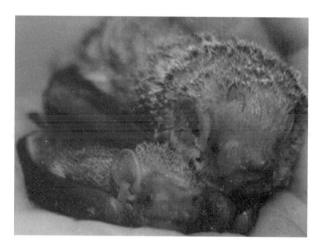

Photo: Amanda Lollar

Red Bat and Pup. *Someone found these bats while mowing his lawn. Mom and baby were treated and released. Amanda reminds people, especially kids, "Never touch a bat."*

In the past five years, Amanda has rehabilitated and released more than 1,000 bats. That's good news for Mineral Wells' mosquito control. Just one Mexican free-tailed bat (Texas' most common species) can eat 3,000-5,000 insects a night!

Bat Chats

Amanda takes four species of bats with her when she gives "Bat Chat" assembly programs in North Central Texas schools. Students are able to see (but not touch) small insect-eating bats and large fruit bats up close and on a TV screen.

Photo: Amanda Lollar

Sunshine II. *Amanda cared for this Mexican free-tail after Sunshine died.*

They learn the importance of leaving wild bats alone and find out the proper steps to take if they find sick or injured bats.

"After spending thousands of hours of watching bats with their gentle, intelligent ways, it's impossible to imagine my life without them," Amanda said. "In many ways they are cleaner and nicer to each other than people are.

"My greatest reward is helping people change their minds about bats. There's no way anyone could see normal bats up close and walk away feeling bad about them."

Photo: Amanda Lollar

Bucko the Bully. *An African straw-colored flying fox bat, Bucko (right), hangs out with his much smaller fruit bat friends.*

Bucko the Klutzy Bat

"The Amazing Bucko" is a favorite attraction for kids visiting Bat World. A buck-toothed African straw-colored flying fox, Bucko likes to stretch out his wings and show off his three-foot wing span.

He was donated by Bat Conservation International (BCI), a well-known organization that researches and protects bats.

"Bucko's so incredibly goofy," Amanda said. "He tries to get into the little fruit bats' roosts for no reason at all, other than the little bats are in there."

The roosts are little wicker baskets that hang upside down. While Bucko is a foot long, the Jamaican fruit bats are only a third his size. So Bucko throws his weight around, swatting at the smaller bats until they leave their baskets. Then he climbs inside their roosts.

"He's such a clown," Amanda said. "Three-fourths of his body hangs out of their baskets."

To pay Bucko back, the little Jamaican fruit bats go by and swat "Bucko's bell," which is a bird bell hanging in the rain forest flight cage.

When Bucko hears them whacking his bell, he shrieks and flies off to defend his territory.

Puttering Around

When Amanda found Putter, an orphaned Mexican free-tail, the little bat was only an inch long, hairless, and full of mites.

"Her legs were clamped up next to her body, and her knees were stiff as a board," Amanda said. "I figured she'd been born breech (feet first) because breech free-tails have a problem with their legs."

Amanda cleaned up the infant bat, made braces for her, and began physical therapy on her legs.

While brushing Putter's fur, Amanda noticed how the bat's legs jerked like a dog's. Brushing then became part of the therapy, helping to build up Putter's weak leg muscles.

Now Putter can move around fairly well, hang upside down, and groom herself all over. She's not strong enough to be released, but since she's used to people and bright lights, Putter will become an education animal.

Soon she'll visit schools and other places, helping more and more people learn about the beauty and benefits of bats.

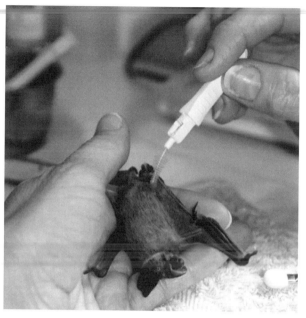

Photo: Amanda Lollar

Kicking Therapy. *When Amanda brushes Putter's fur, the little bat kicks like a dog.*

GREENWOOD WILDLIFE REHABILITATION SANCTUARY

Location:	Longmont, Colorado
Description:	Large center treating more than 2,000 small mammals, birds, and reptiles a year.
Staff:	Two paid staff; more than 125 volunteers
Funding:	Donations, memberships, fundraisers
Newsletter:	*Pinecoon Press,* published 2-4 times a year
Programs:	Many, including interactive picture boards, slide shows, mystery mammal games, portable hospital, and displays
Tours:	Only during open house, held every spring

Photo: Shannon K. Jacobs

Volunteer Rehabilitators. *Ellen Schultz (left) and Jan Bova (right) examine a newly admitted sparrow nestling found under a tree.*

Greenwood was named after the Sanctuary's first patient, a severely burned raccoon. He was rescued from a chimney fire, rehabilitated, and released.

Other critters treated at Greenwood include orphaned and adult coyotes, bats, foxes, squirrels, prairie dogs, turtles, and snakes. Many species of land and water birds also receive care.

Volunteers answer phones, clean cages, chop up food, feed babies, rescue and transport animals, and raise money. In one year, they handled more than 5,000 hotline calls.

Many veterinarians also donate their services, examining and treating sick and injured animals.

Greenwood's newsletter, *Pinecoon Press,* features photos and stories about rescues, treatments, and releases. A special column called "Whatever Happened to ... ?" updates readers on animals described in other issues.

Wildly Popular Programs

Greenwood's education programs reach more than 2,000 people a year. They are especially popular with elementary and middle school students.

Can you imagine a whole class of seventh graders wildly waving their hands in the air, begging to participate in a program?

That's what happened when Ellen Schultz, education coordinator, wheeled her portable hospital and stuffed staff into Broomfield Heights Middle School.

Ellen selected a few lucky volunteers to treat the wild animals she'd brought with her. The animals were stuffed, naturally, but their injuries were based on real cases treated at the Sanctuary.

Photo: Shannon K. Jacobs

Lucky Volunteers. *Using a stuffed fox as model, Ellen Schultz (right) instructs seventh-graders David Fredericks (left) and Shawn Hansen (middle) on how rehabilitators would treat a real injured fox. Greenwood's "Portable Hospital and Stuffed Staff" presentations are a big hit at schools.*

The students learned how to bottle-feed (and burp) raccoon babies, give antibiotic injections to a snake, rescue a prairie dog stuck in a six-pack ring, and help a coyote with a broken leg.

Later, looking like raccoon kits feeling everything with their paws, the eager seventh-graders handled the fascinating display pieces Ellen had set out, including real beaks, talons, skulls, feathers, shells, stuffed bats, and birds' nests. Greenwood has special government permits allowing them to keep these animals parts for education programs.

Photo: Greenwood Wildlife Rehabilitation Sanctuary

Displaced Coyote. *DIA (Denver International Airport) was rescued as a pup, after his burrow was bulldozed during construction of a new airport. DIA was rehabilitated at Greenwood and released, a very wily coyote.*

Humpty Dumpty

Poor Tex. First a car ran over the western box turtle and crushed his shell. Then flies laid eggs in the cracks. By the time Tex was brought to Greenwood, hundreds of *maggots* (fly larvae) were feeding on the turtle's infected flesh.

For days, rehabilitators picked off the maggots, flushed the infected skin, and gave Tex injections of antibiotics. Slowly the turtle's skin began to heal.

A veterinarian used dental acrylic to patch cracks in the turtle's shell. Dental acrylic acts like super glue, keeping the shell in one piece until the damaged tissue can *regenerate* (heal and grow together) on its own.

So, unlike Humpty Dumpty, Tex *was* put back together again. But rehabilitators weren't through with him yet. The next step was to stop him from hibernating.

Photo: *Greenwood Wildlife Rehabilitation Sanctuary*

How Tex Got His Name. *The white dental acrylic patch is shaped like the state of Texas. (Can you guess which state the veterinarian who glued Tex back together again is from?)*

If Tex snoozed through the winter, his body processes would slow down, including the healing of his shell. So rehabilitators kept Tex warm all winter. They fooled the turtle's body into thinking it was summer.

While their human caretakers shivered in snow and ice, Tex and his girlfriend, Painter, lounged around in light and warmth, nibbling melon chunks, carrots, and earthworms, and waiting for spring.

Peanut Pinkies

While trimming a tree, a man found a nest of newborn squirrels inside a cut-off limb. His wife kept the babies warm and took them to Greenwood.

Newborn squirrels are called *pinkies* because they're pink, hairless, and helpless. They're born with eyes and ears closed, and they can't control their body temperature or functions. Without a mother, babies this young (they were two days old) can't survive.

Karen Taylor, animal care coordinator at Greenwood, became the pinkies' foster mother. During the day, she took the tiny babies to the Sanctuary with her. At night, Karen kept them at her home, feeding them every two hours around the clock. They slept in a warm basket.

Two and a half weeks later, the little male died, in spite of all that Karen did to save him. The females did well, though. When their fur started growing in, Karen named them Slick (slicked-back fur on her head) and Kinky (tail fur grew in kinks).

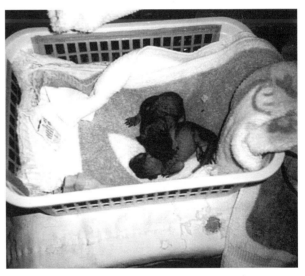

Photo: *Greenwood Wildlife Rehabilitation Sanctuary*

Growing Coats. *These pinky squirrels are starting to grow fur.*

When Kinky and Slick got older, Karen put them in with another squirrel named Twinkie, the victim of a cat attack. The three squirrels raced, leaped, and climbed around the cage like furry little gymnasts.

During one spectacular jump, Slick broke her rear foot. Karen rushed her to the veterinarian for x-rays, worried because hind feet are very important for squirrels' survival. They need them for climbing trees and escaping enemies.

But Slick recovered well, after wearing a tiny cast for awhile and getting a lot of rest.

By the time the scampering squirrels were moved to a bigger outdoor cage, their bodies were covered with thick fur. Wild as the wind, the young rodents didn't want anything to do with humans.

But that didn't hurt Karen's feelings. It meant that she and other Greenwood rehabilitators had done an excellent job of keeping the wild rodents wild.

The three squirrels were released later by their proud foster mom.

Photo: *Greenwood*

Orphaned Fox Kit.

Photo: *Greenwood Sanctuary*

Outa Here!

Photo: *Greenwood Wildlife Rehabilitation Sanctuary*

Fox Release.

CRITTER ALLEY WILDLIFE REHABILITATION CENTER

Location:	Grand Ledge, Michigan
Description:	Large center treating 3,000+ birds and mammals a year
Staff:	Four paid staff; more than 100 volunteers and interns
Funding:	Donations, grants, and fundraisers
Newsletter:	*A Journey with Critter Alley Wildlife Rehabilitation Center,* published 3 times a year
Programs:	School and community education programs
Tours:	No

When Janet Walker was 12 years old, she found a rabbit that had been bitten by a dog. Even the sight of maggots squirming inside the rabbit's open wounds didn't stop Janet from helping the poor creature heal and return to its wild home.

That was more than 40 years ago.

Today, Janet is still helping wildlife return to their homes. She is director of Critter Alley Wildlife Rehabilitation Center, which is located on an eight-acre farm Janet bought in 1988.

Photo: Critter Alley

Still Helping Wildlife. *Janet Walker holds a young woodchuck, the only survivor when a bulldozer tore through her underground nest, killing her family. The woodchuck suffered a broken leg, which was set in a tiny cast. She recovered completely and was released.*

Photo: Critter Alley

Bunny Rescuer. *Janet Walker at 12.*

Among volunteers donating their time at the Center are young people involved in the Junior Volunteer Program.

Headed by two long-term volunteers, the juniors feed and clean the adult animals, groom and exercise education animals, warm bottles, and clean nursery incubators.

Photo: Critter Alley

Walking for Wildlife. Left to right, Terrry Kimball with her two children, Ashley and Dustin Bofysil (and Sebastian the dog), help raise funds for Critter Alley.

Photo: Critter Alley

Young Volunteer. 14-year-old Jennifer Sovey releases orphaned bunnies raised at the Center. Jennifer is an important part of the Junior Volunteer Program.

Junior volunteers also help with fundraising — a very important activity. Can you imagine how much money is needed to care for thousands of animals?

The fundraisers include pop can drives, T-shirt sales, education programs, and bingo games.

Kids from all over Michigan participate in "Walk for Wildlife," the Center's annual fundraiser.

During the winter, Janet travels around the state and presents "Speaking of Wildlife," a program about Michigan's wild backyard neighbors. She advises people on what to do if they find an animal that needs help, and she encourages them to learn about wild animals.

"If I knew each one of you individually, I would appreciate you a lot better than just knowing you as a group," Janet tells her audience.

"It's the same with wildlife. Learn about each species and you will understand and appreciate all animals."

Three's a Charm

A full moon shone on the red fox as she trotted along a hunting trail, a young kit behind her. Lifting her black nose to the sky, the mother fox sniffed the air. Mice — across the road.

108

Quickly she loped ahead, looking back once to make sure the kit was keeping up. Suddenly, a monster roared down the road. Its yellow eyes blinded everything with their powerful beams.

The mother fox froze. She tried to leap across the road, but the car hit her, flinging her lifeless body onto the shoulder. A second later, the young fox slammed down beside her. Whimpering, the kit tried to get up, but she could barely lift her head.

Another car whizzed by, but this one stopped and backed up. The young kit lifted her head again. Her heart thumped in panic — humans! Enemies!

She knew she should run away, as she'd been taught. But the pain in her head and body drained all her energy. She lost consciousness.

The kit never heard the people whispering. She didn't feel them tenderly pick up her broken body and carry it to the car. The people knew about Critter Alley, so they took the young fox there.

Because of their quick action, the young fox was treated immediately for shock, and her life was saved. Later rehabbers discovered that the kit had a broken leg and pelvis as well as a head injury.

By the next day, the fox kit's condition was stable and she was taken to a veterinarian for repair of her broken leg and pelvis. She then returned to Critter Alley for recovery.

Photo: Critter Alley

The little fox improved slowly over the next few days. A few weeks later, a young male fox about the same age was brought to the Center. The two fox kits were put together. They became friends fast, sleeping together wrapped in their bushy white-tipped tails.

Then an adult female fox that had been raised at a nature center was admitted to Critter Alley. Rehabilitators planned to teach her how to be wild so she could be released.

The kits barked with excitement when they saw the adult fox, and the *vixen* (female fox) treated the bright-eyed, romping kits as if they were her own. Together they learned more ways of the wild.

By the end of summer, the black-stockinged trio was ready for release. Rehabilitators set them free in a thick forest surrounded by a lake and open fields. It was paradise for a frisky family of foxes.

Photo: Critter Alley

Good as New. *The rehabilitated young fox was released with her new family.*

109

Leaping for Liberty

Caesar and Sweetie, two bobcats, were admitted to Critter Alley after their owner got evicted from his property. The owner had raised the bobcats for breeding so he could sell the babies.

For years Caesar and Sweetie had lived in tiny, filthy cages. Their only food was pig liver and heart mixed with water once a day. The owner, who was afraid of the bobcats, teased and abused them.

When the bobcats arrived at Critter Alley, Caesar was seven years old. Born in captivity, he'd spent his life being moved from one cramped, muddy cage to another.

Sweetie, who was five years old, had known the wild only briefly when she was young. Then she was captured and caged.

Critter Alley's goal was to rehabilitate the cats and return them to the wild. The first step was to build them new living quarters. Soon each bobcat had a cage big enough to run around and climb in.

Photo: Critter Alley

Bobcat Haven. With a roomy and clean home, good food, and caring people, Sweetie was learning how to be a wild bobcat again.

Then the cats were started on a new diet of road-killed animals. It was the same type of food they'd be eating in the wild.

It took almost two years to teach Caesar and Sweetie the skills they'd need to survive in the wild. They had to learn everything from scratch — how to hunt, hide, chase prey, and stay away from humans.

Finally, it was time for release. Finding the perfect bobcat habitat had taken many months. Twelve volunteers escorted a snarling, spitting Caesar to the release site.

A volunteer opened the cage door, and Caesar stepped out. He sniffed the air and looked around him in wonder. Then, not wasting a second, Caesar bolted for the wild. Free at last!

Photo: Critter Alley

Heading for the Hills. After two years of rehabilitation at Critter Alley, Caesar was set free.

Sadly, Sweetie never left Critter Alley. Because of the abuse she'd suffered over the years, her poor health got worse.

Two months after Caesar sprang into freedom, Sweetie died.

110

More Critter Alley Critters

Photo: Critter Alley

Opossum Release.

Photo: Critter Alley

Apple a Day. *While recovering from a car-hit injury, a beaver enjoys a favorite treat.*

Rehabilitating
Marine Animals

Photo: Doug Franklin

Dramatic Whale Rescue. *Volunteers from The Marine Mammal Conservancy and Wildlife Rescue of the Florida Keys help Tyson, a stranded pilot whale, stay afloat. Volunteers are (left to right) Rosemary Farrell, Eric Watson, and Chris Schulz.*

Chapter 15

Healers at Work

WORKING WITH MARINE ANIMALS

If you've ever jumped into a cold pool or lake, you know how quickly water chills your body — a lot faster than air at the same temperature. Sea animals would chill, too, without thick layers of *blubber* (fat) or dense fur to protect them.

Marine animals burn a lot of energy trying to stay warm. When they don't get enough food, they become weak, cold, and more likely to catch diseases. If pollution or violent storms add more stress to their bodies, survival becomes difficult, if not impossible.

Marine animals are admitted to rehabilitation centers because they're sick, injured, malnourished, or suffering from the effects of severe weather, pollution, or encounters with people. Also, young animals separated from their mothers need human help. Otherwise, they wouldn't survive.

There are special challenges to rehabilitating marine animals. Most are big animals, needing enormous amounts of food and giant holding tanks. They also

©1997 The Marine Mammal Center / Photo: Ken Bach

Separated From Mom. *An orphaned sea lion pup, not old enough to swim on his own, was rescued and taken to The Marine Mammal Center.*

need highly skilled rehabilitators who know their natural history.

Cetaceans (dolphins, whales, and porpoises) have strong family bonds. If rehabilitators want cooperation from family members, they need to understand and respect the animals' family ties.

Conscious Breathing

Another consideration is how marine animals breathe.

"Cetaceans are *conscious breathers*," explained Becky Barron, director of Wildlife Rescue of the Florida Keys

"That means they have to be awake in order to breathe. Humans breathe all the time, even when we're in a coma, or under *anesthesia* (medicine that puts patients to sleep for surgery)."

Because of conscious breathing, surgery is almost out of the question for cetaceans, Becky said. The animals would stop breathing if they received anesthesia, unless they were put on *ventilators* (machines that breathe for patients).

Problems Out of Water

What if a dolphin or sea turtle needs an x-ray? No problem — unless electrical equipment is dropped in the tank of water.

Because of the danger of electric shock to both humans and their patients, marine animals have to be removed from water before electrical equipment can be used.

This is very stressful. Giant animals don't like being hoisted into the air and moved around by cranes.

It also can be dangerous. When they're in water, dolphins and whales are *buoyant* — they float because the water supports their weight.

But when cetaceans are taken out of water, they can squash their own bodies with their massive weight. Sometimes animals injure their internal organs or even suffocate themselves if kept out of water too long.

Freedom for Captive Animals?

If captive marine mammals — those taken from the wild to perform in marine parks and aquariums — are healthy, should they be rehabilitated and released back to the wild?

For years, many dolphins and orcas (killer whales) were taken by force from their families and used for entertainment and research purposes. No one worried about the effects on the captured animal and its family. Now we know a lot more about cetaceans. Their family structures are a lot like ours.

When an orca or dolphin is taken away from its wild home, its family mourns. And the captive creature never stops yearning for its family.

Although there have been several successful releases of rehabilitated cetaceans, some people worry that captive animals will carry diseases to wild populations or that they will starve to death outside marine parks.

Programs for successfully rehabilitating and releasing cetaceans have to include some important steps, according to Rick Trout (Marine Mammal Conservancy in Key Largo, Florida).

"The animals need to be healthy and relatively young," Rick said. "They should spend about a month in protected water near the release site, to get used to the sea. And they should be released in their home waters, where they were first captured."

If captive cougars and bobcats can learn to survive in the wild, why can't cetaceans, which are more intelligent? Should they be given the chance?

What do you think?

THE MARINE MAMMAL CENTER

Location:	Sausalito, California
Description:	Large center treating more than 600 marine mammals a year; many are endangered or threatened
Staff:	35 paid positions, including veterinarians, biologists, vet techs, and educators; 800 volunteers
Funding:	Memberships, donations, fundraisers, gift shop
Newsletter:	*The Release*
Programs:	Many — at The Center and off site
Tours:	Yes, at The Center and PIER 39 Interpretive Center; two gift shops, one at each location

©*1997 The Marine Mammal Center/Photo: Ken Bach*

Making a Splash. *TMMC volunteers help an elephant seal pup into a pool.*

The Marine Mammal Center (TMMC) was started in the 1970s. Then, it was a tiny operation run by volunteers who transported sick and injured animals in the back seats of their cars and fed the animals at night by the light of car headlights.

Today, TMMC is the largest marine mammal rehabilitation center in the country. Located on seven acres of land, The Center is made up of a veterinary hospital with animal pens and pools, an intensive care unit, laboratories, and offices. Veterinarians, veterinary technicians, biologists, educators, and volunteers work there.

In addition to the main hospital staff, TMMC has rescue teams stationed along the California coast. Volunteers care for sick or injured animals at two holding places until they can be transferred to the main center.

Last year, more than 600 marine animals — seals, sea lions, whales, dolphins and sea otters — were rehabilitated at The Center. More than 800 volunteers assisted in all areas of rehabilitation. Members (35,000) and donors provided most of the financial support.

© 1997 The Marine Mammal Center / Photo: Jane Oka

Van Gogh. *Notice the scars? This California sea lion was caught in a fishing net that wound too tighly around his head and neck. Like his famous namesake, Van Gogh lost an ear (flap).*

Research

In addition to rescue and rehabilitation, TMMC conducts some very important research. Scientists study marine mammal diseases, animal behavior and nutrition, and the effects of pollution and severe weather on ocean mammals.

The Center also participates in California's oil response program. Staff and volunteers are active in helping to protect critical coastal habitat.

Hands-on Education

Wouldn't it be fun to learn about the natural history of sea lions while watching hundreds of wild sea lions climb onto the floating docks at PIER 39 in San Francisco's Fisherman's Wharf? That's one of the many education programs offered by TMMC.

Classes are taught also at The Center, and instructors visit schools and communities, sometimes traveling in TMMC's Sea Van, the "classroom on wheels."

The Center educators inform people about the marine world and how to protect it. All education programs are available in Spanish.

The Center also offers guided coastal outings, which include taking beach walks, exploring tide pools, and watching whales from the shore.

Helping Humphrey

People couldn't believe their eyes when they spotted a humpback whale in San Francisco Bay in 1985. Gliding under the Golden Gate Bridge, the whale (named Humphrey) swam through two more bays and under three more bridges.

For the next three weeks, Humphrey cruised up the Sacramento River in fresh water that became more and more shallow. Everyone who saw him worried that the giant would *beach* (get stuck on the bottom). Weighing in at 40 tons, Humphrey definitely was too big for a river!

The Marine Mammal Center rescue team worked with hundreds of other volunteers to save Humphrey. At first rescuers banged on pipes, making loud noises underwater to drive the whale back toward the bay.

Once in the bay, rescuers played recordings of humpback whales feeding. That was music to Humphrey!

He followed the boat across the bay, under the Golden Gate Bridge, and into the Pacific Ocean. The wayward whale was saved.

118

The Return of Humphrey

In 1990, Humphrey swam into San Francisco Bay again, heading inland. This time he got stuck in the mud.

TMMC's rescue team and medical experts worked frantically to free Humphrey. After three exhausting days and nights, they saved him. The huge whale glided back into the Pacific Ocean.

No one knows what has happened to the wandering whale since then. Many people expected a repeat performance in 1995, since Humphrey seemed to return every five years.

In the spring of that year a whale that looked like Humphrey was spotted in Baja, California. That whale wisely stayed away from San Francisco Bay.

©*1997 The Marine Mammal Center/Photo: Ken Bach*

Stuck in the Mud. *Three TMMC staff members evaluate Humphrey's condition while the unfortunate humpback whale is beached. The staff is (left to right): Jan Roletto, curator; Ken Lee, stranding coordinator; and Laurie Gage, veterinarian.*

An Otterly Bad Hair Day

Jambo, an endangered California sea otter, wasn't doing well on his own. Recently *weaned* (not nursing), the young otter was cold and thin, and his fur was matted. He was rescued and taken to The Marine Mammal Center.

Otters are the only marine animals without blubber. Instead, they have two layers of dense fur.

Otter fur — with about one million hairs per square inch — is the thickest of all mammal fur. (Human hair is only about 1/8 as dense as otter fur.)

When an otter rolls in the water, air gets trapped between the two layers of fur. The air is like a wet suit, holding in the otter's body heat.

Otters need to *groom* (clean) themselves constantly to keep their fur free of food and dirt. If the fur gets matted, it can't fluff up and trap air. Then it loses its ability to repel water.

Jambo was kept in a *tote* (portable pen) with a pool of water that could be covered to keep him out. Because his fur was in such miserable shape, he chilled quickly, so Jambo was allowed only quick dips in the cool water. (Warm water can't be used with otters because it damages their fur.)

Each time Jambo came out of the water, rehabilitators had to dry him off and warm him under a lamp.

In the wild, otters burn many calories staying warm. To fuel all that energy, they eat constantly, just as Jambo did.

©1997 The Marine Mammal Center/Photo: Ken Bach

Seafood Snacks. *Jambo, an endangered California sea otter, eats in his pool at TMMC.*

Exhausted rehabilitators had to let Jambo into his pool every few hours around the clock to eat. Why did Jambo eat in the pool? Because otters usually eat floating on their backs in the water. Using their chests as tables, they hammer clams, mussels, and other shellfish with rocks.

Each time Jambo finished a seafood meal, the staff supervised his grooming, making sure his fur was thoroughly cleaned. They knew that without good grooming habits, Jambo would not survive in the wild.

With all the skilled attention he got, Jambo improved quickly. In preparation for release, he was moved to a large pool and given live food.

A few weeks later, Jambo was released to his Morro Bay home, where he now lives an otterly well-groomed life.

MANATEE HOSPITAL

Location:	Lowry Park Zoo in Tampa, Florida
Description:	The only nonprofit hospital in the world dedicated to rehabilitating sick, injured, and orphaned manatees
Staff:	Zoo staff and volunteers
Funding:	Lowry Park Zoo budget; private donations; 8% of money from Florida manatee license tags (1996)
Newsletter:	Yes, with zoo membership
Programs:	Educational exhibits with live manatees; kids' sleepovers
Tours:	Yes, as part of Lowry Park Zoo admission

In 1972, the West Indian Manatee was placed on the Endangered Species List. Today, there are only about 2,000 manatees left in the wild.

That's why the Manatee Hospital is a such an important place. It provides rehabilitation for individual animals, research studies to learn more about protecting the species, and vital education for the public.

Mystery Disease

During the spring of 1996, more than 150 manatees died from a mysterious illness. State and federal scientists worked frantically to identify the cause.

As the only center treating sick, live animals, the Manatee Hospital cared for anywhere from 13-15 manatees at once.

Zoo vets began to notice dramatic improvements in many of the animals after they'd been given round-the-clock care and kept in clean water for a few days. These observations helped identify the cause of the manatee die-off — *red tide.*

Red tide is discolored sea water caused by blooming *algae* (tiny sea plants). In large concentrations, red tide is toxic to marine animals.

It affects their nervous systems and causes muscle spasms and paralysis. Animals may drown if not rescued.

Photo: Dale Moore

Manatee Emergency Room. *Lowry Park Zoo's animal care staff receives a manatee suffering from the effects of red tide.*

Because manatees reproduce slowly, they won't survive as a species if too many animals die off at once. Natural disasters, as well as human activities, keep manatees in constant danger of *extinction* (existing no more).

The gentle sea cows spend a lot of time in shallow water, feeding on sea grass and other plants. They have to surface to breathe, and that's when they're often hit by speeding boats.

Nearly all adults have slash scars from boat propellers. Loud boats also disrupt the animals' mating rituals and social gatherings.

PROTECTING MANATEES

Florida has taken steps to help its official state mammal. There are now 22 "protection zones," which are places where manatees normally gather. Boats must go slowly through these zones from November 15 through March 31.

Photo: Shannon K. Jacobs

Scarred for Life. *Most manatees have slash scars from speed boat propellers.*

Habitat destruction, waterway gates, pollution, and cold weather also injure and kill manatees. Because they can't survive for long in water cooler than 68 degrees, manatees spend winters in Florida, usually in warm natural springs or by hydroelectric plants.

Sometimes, though, even Florida gets hit with chilly winters, and that means trouble for manatees. Some, especially the younger ones, develop life-threatening *hypothermia* (low body temperature).

The Manatee Hospital has rehabilitated 30 manatees since it opened in 1991. It has x-ray and ultrasound equipment, an operating room, veterinary offices, and three large rehabilitation pools.

The Hospital is located behind the scenes of the Manatee and Aquatic Center at Lowry Park Zoo, where more than half a million people visit the manatee exhibit every year.

While the visitors watch live sea cows forage for carrots and lettuce in underwater viewing tanks, they learn how to protect these endangered animals and their habitat.

Costly Manatee Program

Taking care of manatees is expensive. Half of the Zoo's annual animal department budget is spent on manatee rehabilitation.

Food for just one manatee costs $27,000 a year. To keep properly filtered water in the tanks at 74 degrees, the Hospital uses 100 gallons of propane and $160 worth of electricity every day.

122

Photo: Richard Wilhelm

Special Manatee Pools. *Lowry Park Zoo's Manatee Rehabilitation Center has a series of interconnecting pools. Up to 16 manatees can be held and treated at one time. Shift gates allow zoo vets to move animals from pool to pool or to quarantine them, if needed.*

Manatee Hospital staff and Amber Wildlife, a volunteer group, transport recovered manatees to release sites. Manatees are so popular in Florida that often several hundred people line up along the river banks to welcome the sea cows home.

Starting Anew

Newbob, an orphaned baby manatee, got his name from the man who found him (Bob) and the day he was rescued (New Year's Day). Newbob's mother had been crushed and killed in a *lock* (gate that opens and closes waterways) in Lake Okeechobee.

When admitted, Newbob weighed only 129 pounds, and he wouldn't eat. He was sent to Homosassa Springs, a wildlife park and sanctuary for manatees. The staff hoped that one of two nursing females at the Springs would become Newbob's foster mother, but that didn't happen. Newbob returned to the Hospital.

Public Support Needed

How can people help the Manatee Hospital?

"Visit the Zoo and learn all you can about manatees," suggested Sam Winslow, Lowry Park's directory of collections. "People also can adopt a manatee for $35 or more. If you can't contribute money, you can always volunteer at the Zoo."

Volunteer divers help by vacuuming the manatee tanks every morning. This saves the paid staff at least two hours a day.

Photo: Shannon K. Jacobs

Manatee Sanctuary. *Manatees are fed well at Homosassa Springs.*

The following spring, Newbob went to Merritt Island, a 240-acre National Wildlife Refuge located on Florida's east coast. It serves as a halfway house for manatees. They learn how to *forage* (search) for their natural foods in the sea water.

Once again, Newbob's fickle appetite let him down, so back to the Hospital he went. The staff gave him lots of lettuce, carrots, and high protein biscuits, fattening him up to 1100 pounds.

Photo: Richard Wilhelm

Great Success Story. *Lucky Frank works on his appetite while healing from cold water stress. He arrived at Manatee Hospital in February of 1996 and was released a year later, in the spring.*

Lucky Frank

For a while, Newbob shared a pool with Lucky Frank, a juvenile manatee admitted with hypothermia.

Weak and underweight when rescued, Lucky Frank had developed several infections. After successfully treating the infections, the Hospital staff focused on Lucky Frank's poor eating habits.

They put the two young manatees together, hoping Newbob would influence Lucky Frank.

It worked! Inspired by his older friend, Lucky Frank became a hearty consumer of lettuce, and his weight increased.

Meanwhile, Newbob continued to improve. Both manatees recovered so well that they were released together.

The Zoo staff was hoping they two sea cow pals would stay together, but Lucky Frank headed upstream on his own.

Newbob was fitted with a satellite tracking belt so his progress could be followed. Dr. David Murphy, Lowry Park Zoo veterinarian, caught up with Newbob in the wild and drew a blood sample.

Lab results showed just what the Hospital staff was hoping — Newbob is healthy and doing well in his wild home.

TEXAS STATE AQUARIUM

Location: Corpus Christi, Texas
Description: Large 7.3 acre center on the beach, with exhibits and re-created habitats; 150 animals treated a year
Staff: 80 paid staff; 300 volunteers
Funding: Memberships, admission fees, programs, donations
Newsletter: *Star*, members' quarterly newsletter
Programs: Daily and educational; on and off site
Tours: Available

The Gladys Sue Albertson Memorial Rehabilitation program at the Texas State Aquarium (TSA) is the only program on the Texas coast dedicated to treating birds, sea turtles, and marine mammals.

Nonreleasable animals are used in daily programs to educate people about the dangers the animals face and how people can help them.

TSA has exciting exhibits showing sea life in the Gulf of Mexico. One of them, "Turtle Bend," is an artificial turtle habitat. It serves as a home for sick, orphaned, and injured sea turtles.

Currently, six turtles (including an endangered Kemp's ridley) live inside the exhibit tank, and several others are being treated behind the scenes.

Two of the rehabilitating turtles are olive ridley hatchlings, which are cousins to Kemp's ridleys. They were brought to TSA after hatching at the Dallas Zoo. The eggs had been confiscated from a woman who tried to sneak them illegally into the U.S. from Central America.

When the sea turtle babies are big enough to survive on their own, they'll be released in waters off Costa Rica.

Sea Turtle Research

One of the Aquarium's research projects involves tracking sea turtles. The project aims to teach students about sea turtles as well as to increase the population of Kemp's ridleys.

Photo: Helen Swetman

Turtle Bend. *Young visitors watch sea turtles during the 1995 grand opening of Texas State Aquarium's re-created turtle habitat.*

Teachers and students from area high schools help collect information on several Kemp's ridleys, which are fitted with satellite transmitters.

The teachers and students traveled to the ridleys' only known remaining nesting place in Mexico, where they helped protect eggs, release hatchlings, and tag more turtles for the next study.

School and community groups are welcome to tour the Aquarium's 7.3 acres. TSA educators visit schools, using slide shows, theater productions, and hands-on marine displays to teach about life in the sea and how humans affect it.

A mobile exhibit, "Ocean in Motion," takes the Gulf of Mexico to thousands of schools around the state. The Aquarium also hosts SeaCamp, a marine science day camp for kids 6 -15, and a live satellite show called "Wonders Under the Sea."

East Coast Turtle

A juvenile Kemp's ridley sea turtle named Snapper was hit by a speed boat off the coast of New York.

Photo: Helen Swetman

Sea Turtle. *A Kemp's ridley turtle.*

Because of permanent injuries, the sea turtle can't survive in the wild, so the Aquarium is his permanent home.

Stranded in the Lone Star State

More than 120 dolphins washed ashore along the Texas coast in 1994. Most of them died. A few live animals were treated at the Texas State Aquarium.

Volunteers from TSA and the Texas Marine Mammal Stranding Network (part of a national volunteer group) stayed with the dolphins day and night.

They swam the animals around holding tanks, trying to keep their *blowholes* (holes for breathing, located near or on top of a dolphin's head) above water so the dolphins wouldn't drown.

One young male Atlantic bottlenose dolphin named Double Trouble arrived at the Aquarium. Like the other dolphins, he suffered from a respiratory infection. But he improved quickly and began swimming on his own.

Soon Double Trouble was strong enough to be a candidate for release — a very rare situation for a *stranded* marine animal. An animal is considered stranded when it goes into shallow water or other water where it normally wouldn't go and seems to be in distress. Usually, animals are so sick or injured by the time they strand that they don't recover.

Double Trouble was tagged with a satellite tracking device that allowed researchers to follow his movements in the wild. Then he was loaded by stretcher into a box especially designed for him. Volunteers moved Double Trouble onto a truck and ferried him across a channel.

They then lifted the box by crane onto a research boat. The boat motored 10 miles offshore, where the crane lowered Double Trouble into the water. He was released.

Setting a Record

Double Trouble set a record that day. He was the first dolphin in Texas history to survive a stranding, go through rehabilitation, and get released.

At that time, only four such dolphin rehabilitations and releases had taken place in the United States.

Prevention Is Critical

Few marine mammals survive strandings, even with excellent rehabilitation care. Would they be better protected if we all worked to prevent pollution, which may be responsible for making some animals sick and causing them to strand?

Photo: Helen Swetman

Double Trouble. *A Texas Marine Mammal Stranding Network volunteer feeds Double Trouble during the dolphin's stay at TSA's rehabilitation and education facility, Sea Lab.*

WILDLIFE RESCUE OF THE FLORIDA KEYS

Location:	Key West, Florida
Description:	Medium-sized center treating native Florida wildlife, including marine animals
Staff:	Director and volunteers
Funding:	Memberships, donations, fundraisers
Newsletter:	Yes
Programs:	Yes, at the Center; for young people and some adults
Tours:	By appointment

Photo: Shannon K. Jacobs

Fish Food. Becky Barron cuts up fish to feed gulls, pelicans, and other birds at the wildlife center.

Like many rehabilitators, Becky Barron began her wildlife work as a veterinary technician.

Presently, as director of Wildlife Rescue, she assists with dolphin and whale rescues. She also supervises the rehabilitation of more than a thousand land mammals, birds, and reptiles every year.

Wildlife Rescue offers several hands-on educational programs for kids. One of them, "Kids and Critters Club," is for 7-11 year olds. The weekly program mixes environmental activities with hands-on care of animals. Kids help prepare the animals' food, feed a few of the calm critters, and help with bandages.

"The kids wear hard hats, so if the hawks jump around, they don't get scratched," Becky explained. "We have vultures here, too. It's quite an experience for kids to be that close to an animal that's usually just a black speck in the sky."

Piloting the Whales

Becky was among three thousand volunteers who helped rescue four pilot whales that stranded near her home in Big Pine Key in 1995.

The whales were too sick to swim. Volunteers worked in four-hour shifts, holding them up to keep them from sinking and drowning.

128

The adult female whale was named Kandi, after the young woman who pulled her from the sea bottom. Kandi's juvenile son was named Tyson (after boxer Mike Tyson) because of all his scars.

The other two males included a frisky juvenile orphan dubbed Dennis (as in Dennis the Menace) and Elvis, who probably was Kandi's mate.

This was the first time in U.S. history that whales were rehabilitated by volunteers in open water, according to Rick Trout, director of husbandry at Marine Mammal Conservancy (MMC) in Key Largo.

Photo: Chris Schulz

Elvis. *Volunteers hold Elvis firmly while other whales are being treated.*

Photo: Doug Franklin

Floating the Whales. *Volunteers near Key West hold up a stranded pilot whale to keep it from drowning.*

Volunteers from MMC and Wildlife Rescue of the Florida Keys joined together to coordinate the rescue, rehabilitation, and release of the whales.

One of the major challenges of working with the whales in open water was ensuring that every person knew what to do.

Nearly 100 volunteers a day had to be quickly trained. Rick and Becky supervised volunteers, tube-fed and medicated the whales, and regularly drew blood to check the health of the animals.

"The most life-threatening situation was *dehydration* (loss of body fluids)," explained Lynne Stringer, MMC animal care technician. "The animals were exposed to sun and not eating fish, which is where they usually get their fluids."

The whales were tube-fed blenderized "fish shakes" three times a day. After gently prying open a whale's mouth, Becky and Lynne inserted a garden hose-sized tube into the first stomach compartment (whales have three stomach compartments).

Then they poured in the fish gruel. Not surprisingly, the whales disliked the tubings. Even sick pilot whales could easily injure or kill people, yet these animals hurt no one. Why were they so cooperative? Becky gave most of the credit to Rick, who is a former dolphin trainer.

"We spent half the time nursing these animals and half the time learning what was acceptable behavior in dealing with different family members," she said. "Rick taught the rest of us to be constantly aware of things, such as a whale giving a little tap with a pectoral fin or moving its body in a certain way, warning you not to do something."

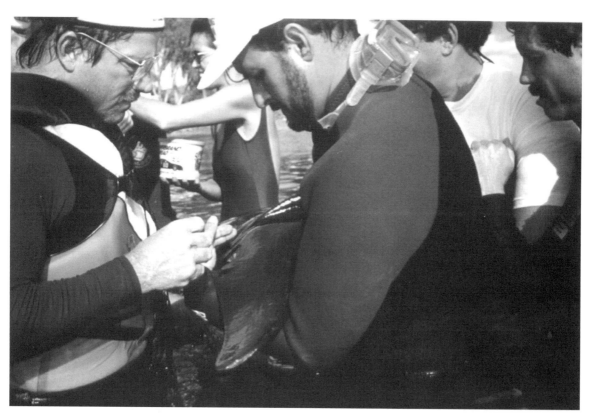

Photo: Doug Franklin

A Way With Whales. Rick Trout's understanding of marine mammals helped create a safe experience for all. Rick Trout (left) and Robert Lingenfelser (middle), MMC president, draw blood from a whale. To their right is volunteer John Powers.

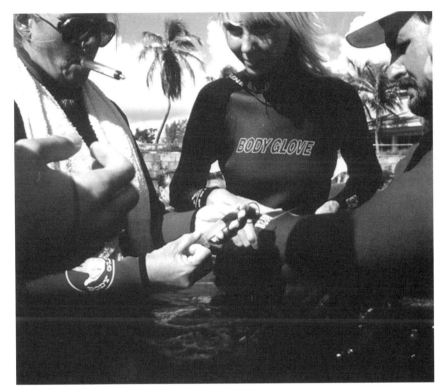

Blood Tests. *From left to right, Becky Barron, Lynne Stringer, MMC animal care technician, and Robert Lingenfelser, MMC president, draw blood from a whale.*

Photo: Doug Franklin

When the whales got stronger, they were moved to a nearby, unused boat basin with deeper water. Volunteers wore float jackets to stay up. They kept the whales afloat by holding strips of foam under them like waterwings.

Volunteers sprayed the whales with ice water to keep them from overheating. They also gave the animals physical therapy, swimming them and massaging their muscles.

The community of Big Pine Key generously pitched in. Some people volunteered as whale rescuers. Others provided supplies, food, tents, and portable toilets for the thousands of helpers.

Luckily, the whales had stranded near a resort. Owners of the Mariner Resort let exhausted volunteers take showers and nap in vacant rooms.

Losing Friends

The whales were eating better by the second week. Then tragedy struck.

Dennis, the 450-pound juvenile, dived too deeply one day while playing in a canal, and got stuck in the mud. Before he could be rescued, Dennis inhaled some of the mud. He soon died of pneumonia.

A week later, Elvis developed complications from a lung infection and died. The deaths were hard for the surviving whales as well as the humans. Kandi and Tyson lost their appetites and energy.

Slowly, they began to improve. Volunteers showered them with encouragement and attention.

Ready for Release

Finally, after two months of treatment, Kandi and Tyson were ready for release. First they were tagged and *freeze-branded* (a painless tattoo, used for identification). Then the whales were loaded onto a 74-foot U.S. Navy landing craft.

Special cushioned stretchers held up the 700-pound Tyson and his 1,000-pound mother. The ship took the marine mammals and 40 volunteers 15 miles out to sea, where the whales were released.

Three days later Kandi and Tyson were spotted from the air, swimming and feeding with a pod of dolphins.

Photo: Chris Schulz

Delicate Cargo. *A U.S. Navy landing craft prepares to load volunteers and whales.*

Photo: Chris Schulz

Going in Style. *Tyson rests on a special waterbed aboard the ship. Volunteer Chris Schulz keeps him cool with towels soaked in ice water. In the next bed, Tyson's mother, Kandi, gets the same treatment.*

Photo: Doug Franklin

Rescued, Rehabilitated, and Released. *Kandi and Tyson were saved because of thousands of brave, skillful, and dedicated people who assisted in their recovery.*

Strandings

Nobody knows exactly why whales strand. The animals could be sick, old, confused, or full of parasites. Pollution may be making some animals sick.

"Scientists are finding toxins in the body tissues of a lot of dead marine mammals," Becky said. "We find toxins in many of the animals we work with."

One of Rick Trout's theories is that stranding is a protection against drowning.

"Whales are as frightened of drowning as humans are," he explained. "That's why they go to beaches when they get sick, instead of heading into deep waters."

Whatever the reason, Rick and Becky agreed that stranded animals should not be pushed off shore. "Whales strand for a reason," Becky said. "Rarely do they make a wrong turn and come 15 miles into shore. They probably need treatment."

Helping Stranded Animals

"If you see a stranded whale, call the Coast Guard or Marine Patrol right away," Becky suggested. "They'll contact qualified people to check the animals. They'll also explain what you can do until the experts arrive."

133

Rehabilitating Birds

Photo: Karen Von den Deale

Screechers. Juvenile screech owls with three different personalities were rehabilitated at WILD CARE, Inc., on Cape Cod.

Chapter 16

Healers at Work

WORKING WITH BIRDS

Just as some mammals fatten up for hibernation, many birds eat like crazy, too. But they don't hibernate. They migrate.

Migration

Over 80% of birds that breed in North America migrate. In the fall, birds travel thousands of miles, often to Central and South America where the weather is warm and food is abundant.

Donna Clement

In the spring, many birds wing northward to Canada and Alaska to nest and raise their young.

On any spring or autumn night, millions of birds fly over the United States. Scientists know this because they've watched through telescopes focused on the moon and counted birds flying past.

Some birds travel at night, some in the daytime, and a few do both.

Although each species has its own route, birds generally follow four U.S. migration *flyways* (paths or lanes which are most heavily traveled): the Atlantic, Mississippi, Central (Great Plains and Rocky Mountains), and Pacific.

Migration is filled with dangers every wingbeat of the way. Because birds cross state and country lines, they may go from being protected in one area to being hunted in another.

They often face storms, headwinds that sap their energy, and predators that capture or kill them.

Risky Rest Stops

While a few birds travel nonstop to their destinations, many rest in stopover places. That's how people in Connecticut might see tropical birds migrating from South America.

These rest stops are very important for migrating birds. But they also can be risky places.

Tired and hungry birds sometimes discover that the trees they rested in the year before are gone, replaced by homes or shops. Their water sources may be dried up. In some places, birds get shot out of the sky for target practice, attacked by cats, or poisoned.

Photo: Michael Judish

Poisoned. *Like many hungry, migrating raptors, this eagle ate a dead animal. But the carcass had been poisoned to kill predators such as coyotes.*

Birds also get trapped in six-pack ring holders or fishing line while swimming or bathing in water. A few migrating water birds have landed on what they thought was water from the air. Too late they discovered it was a shiny, wet parking lot.

Habitat Loss Tragedy

Habitats at both ends of migration routes are shrinking as people cut down forests and drain wetlands.

When waterways shrink, more water birds are forced to share space. This makes the threat of disease more serious. One sick duck can infect a lake full of waterfowl.

Recently, scientists have documented that the numbers of some songbirds and other migrating birds are declining. This may be due to hazards the birds face during migration as well as shrinking habitats.

If birds haven't put on enough fat before migration, they lose strength and can't keep up with their flock. The young, sick, and injured sometimes can't keep up either. These are the birds that often end up with rehabilitators.

Rehabilitators work with many kinds of birds. Some specialize in certain species such as raptors, water birds, and even tiny, jeweled hummingbirds.

Photo: Urban Wildlife Rescue

Hummingbird Feeding*.*

ALASKA RAPTOR REHABILITATION CENTER

Location:	Sitka, Alaska
Description	Large center treating 200-300 raptors and other birds a year
Staff:	Seven paid staff members; 250 volunteers from all over the world donate 20,000 hours annually
Funding:	Donations, memberships, bird adoptions, classes, grants, and gift shop sales
Programs:	Yes, at the Center, in schools, and around the country
Newsletter:	*The Mew Review*, published quarterly
Tours:	Yes (please call ahead); also sets up tours with cruise ships that visit Sitka in summers

Photo: Kim Heacox

Buddies. *Dick Griffin, ARRC director, with Buddy, a permanent resident bald eagle, at an education pro-*

At the Alaska Raptor Rehabilitation Center (ARRC), all the birds are named.

"Our volunteers give them names, usually within three days," Director Dick Griffin explained. "We think it helps volunteers feel ownership in the birds' care."

ARRC also allows visitors to view some of the raptors. Dick said, "People can see the birds with permanent disabilities, because they're used for education and display, but birds being rehabilitated for release are isolated from the public."

ARRC was started in 1980 by a group of individuals concerned about protecting raptors. Like many rehabilitators, these people started in someone's back yard.

The Center is located on 17 acres. Most of the patients are bald eagles. In 1997, ARRC admitted 81 injured eagles and more than 100 other birds.

The birds are exercised in a 160-foot flight barn. The large space enables the birds to build up their flight muscles.

Unlike many other centers, ARRC allows children to volunteer, as long as they're under the control of their parents or guardians. In fact, more and more families are choosing to spend vacations at the Center, volunteering their time.

139

Many home-schooled children visit the Center with their families to learn more about science and nature.

Programs for Families

ARRC provides several programs for all family members. "Alaska Wildlife Adventure" is offered every spring and fall. It's a seven-day program that enables people to learn about eagles by interacting with live birds.

"Roosting with Raptors," another education program, is a sleep-over at the Center. Kids learn about raptors, make masks, and explore the outside river area and wetlands.

For bald eagle education, ARRC has an education room complete with a traveling trunk, which is taken into Alaska classrooms. The trunk holds real eagle parts, activities, and lots of hands-on projects dealing with raptors.

The Center has designed an ARRC Passport for students on field trips or summer tours. Using the Passport as a guide that moves them from one area of the Center to another, students check off activities as they complete them. Each finished page is stamped.

When kids finish the whole series, their passport photos are taken with an ARRC bird.

The Teaching Eagle

One of ARRC's most popular and beloved birds was a bald eagle named Buddy. A nonreleasable education bird, Buddy traveled around the country with staff members, visiting schools and communities.

Buddy couldn't be released because he was human-imprinted. When he was an eaglet, Buddy either fell from his nest or was stolen. The people who raised Buddy didn't know much about baby raptors, because they let the young eagle imprint on them. Then they abandoned him in an Alaskan village.

Maybe they didn't know how helpless he was, or maybe they figured he would do what eagles do "naturally" — hunt. That's where they were wrong. Birds aren't born knowing how to hunt and fish. They have to learn those skills from their parents.

After he was abandoned, Buddy walked around the village for weeks, begging for food. He was starving, because he was used to being fed by people. In fact, Buddy thought he *was* people.

One day, Buddy tried to snatch a red ball away from a child. He may have thought the ball was food, or he may have been trying to hunt or play.

Photo: Kari Gabriel

Buddy at School. *Buddy made friends all over the country when he visited schools and communities.*

Although Buddy didn't hurt the child, he scared him and the boy's parents. They knew what razor-sharp talons could do to a child. The parents called the police and reported a dangerous eagle attacking a child.

Buddy, the criminal eagle, was picked up and taken to ARRC, where rehabilitators fed him and cared for him. One thing they couldn't fix, though was his most serious injury — imprinting.

As Buddy *matured* (grew older) into adulthood, his dark head and tail feathers turned white.

Photo: Amy Sweeney

Maturing Buddy. *As Buddy got older, his dark head and tail feathers turned white.*

His behavior began to change, too. He began building nests with sticks and grass and defending the nests, as mature eagles do in the wild. When he chose a human rehabilitator as a mate, it was clear how serious the human-imprinting was.

In 1995, while on a tour in Los Angeles, Buddy died of a sudden illness. The beautiful eagle had traveled all over the country and made many friends in his short life. Buddy's magnificent presence reminded people everywhere that all wild creatures deserve to be healthy and free.

A Whale of a Spill

Bonnie and Clyde, two hungry, young bald eagles, climbed inside a dead whale to feast on the meat. They didn't think much about the oil greasing up their feathers.

After they had filled their bellies, the eagles prepared for flight. They discovered they were grounded.

Twenty other eagles who also had been feeding on the whales died before they could be rescued. Because their feathers were oiled, the birds couldn't fly or stay warm. The dead eagles were found near the whale carcass.

Bonnie and Clyde were lucky, though. Both eagles were taken to ARRC for rehabilitation. Clyde recovered quickly in two months, but Bonnie had trouble flying.

"She had everything working right," Dick Griffin explained. "She'd fly horizontally (across) but not vertically (up and down).

"We put her through a vertical exercise program. That's something we usually don't have to do, because one thing a bird wants to do is get up and go."

Photo: Harvey and Pamela Hergett

Bonnie. *The young bald eagle had trouble flying at first, during rehabilitation.*

Photo: Harvey and Pamela Hergett

Clyde. *Recovering quickly, Clyde was released before Bonnie.*

The program worked. Bonnie finally was released to Alaskan skies. In a few years, Bonnie will choose a mate. If she stays away from dead whales, traps, guns, small planes, and power lines, she'll be able to enjoy a wild life for many years.

SUNCOAST SEABIRD SANCTUARY

Location:	Near St. Petersburg, Florida
Description:	Large wild bird rehabilitation center treating more than 7,000 birds a year; most are water birds
Staff:	20 full-time staff; three volunteer vets; many volunteers
Funding:	Donations, memberships, fundraisers, and corporate sponsors
Newsletter:	*Suncoast Seabird Sanctuary,* published quarterly
Programs:	Guided tours of center; monthly education programs
Tours:	Yes; open 7 days a week, 9 am to dark; free admission

Photo: Shannon K. Jacobs

A Friend of Birds. *Ralph Heath holds a disabled brown pelican that lives at Suncoast Seabird Sanctuary. The bird is blind in one eye.*

Stopping to help a cormorant with a broken wing changed the life of Ralph Heath in 1971. It also made the world a better place for birds.

Ralph took the bird to a veterinarian, who pinned the broken wing. Naming the bird Maynard, Ralph took him home to recover.

Cormorants eat a lot of fish. Luckily, local bait shop owners generously donated food for Maynard.

When word got out about Ralph's healing touch, people began bringing him injured birds. Sometimes up to 80 birds a day were dropped off at his home clinic.

History of Helping

Being around injured animals wasn't new to Ralph. Years before, he and other kids had taken hurt creatures to Ralph's father, an orthopedic surgeon.

"My father's office was in Tampa," Ralph explained. "When kids brought him injured animals, he'd keep them in boxes and operate on them if they needed it. I'd come home from school and watch him operate on the animals — squirrels, rabbits, turtles, and birds."

In 1972, Ralph turned his beach home into the Suncoast Seabird Sanctuary. Since then it's grown into the largest wild bird hospital in the U.S.

A team of wildlife biologists, veterinary technicians, and volunteers rehabilitate and release about 7,000 birds a year.

Suncoast Seabird Sanctuary is located on beachfront land on the Gulf of Mexico, where visitors can stroll around the sunny acre-and-a-half. Thirty large *aviaries* (enclosures for birds) are homes for birds that can't be released as well as those being prepared for release.

On the drawing board is a 2,800-square-foot wildlife hospital. It will have laboratory and x-ray rooms, several stations for washing oiled birds, an operating room, and a recovery/intensive care room.

Every day, 15-20 seabirds, land birds, or birds of prey are brought to the Sanctuary. Sometimes 500 birds at one time live and recover there.

Photo: Stan Ashbrook

Birds of Prey. *Raptors, such as these barn owls, come to the Sanctuary from all over Florida.*

The birds eat more than 500 pounds of fish, fruits, nuts, and meat a day. The annual cost of fish alone is $75,000!

Disabled Birds Thrive

Although Maynard the cormorant lived, he wasn't able to fly again. Ralph got the proper permits so he could give the bird a home for the rest of his life.

Many other disabled birds live at the Sanctuary now with others of their species. Some have reproduced in captivity, and others have gone to zoos for captive breeding programs.

Photo: Shannon K. Jacobs

Rehabilitation Compound. *Recovering brown pelicans are evaluated before release. In order to survive in the wild, they must be able to fly and catch fish.*

By offering a home for permanently disabled birds that reproduce, the Sanctuary has added many healthy birds to declining wild flocks.

More than 600 threatened brown pelican babies have been hatched by captive parents and eventually released.

Exciting Education Programs

Free education programs are offered at the Sanctuary on the first Sunday of each month. The programs are presented by Sanctuary staff, veterinarians, and other experts in their fields. Topics have included environmental awareness, bird identification, wildlife photography, and workshops for those who want to help rescue wild birds.

Helping Hooked Birds

An ongoing education effort at the Sanctuary is teaching people how to help hooked birds. The 100,000 people who visit the place each year learn how to prevent hooking injuries.

"Amateur fishermen in Florida cause most of the injuries," Ralph Heath explained. "They aren't used to birds like brown pelicans that hang around people and dive for their food."

When brown pelicans catch a fish that's been hooked, the hook can snag them. Water birds also get caught in fishing line that people throw away or lose.

The line can wrap around a leg or wing, trapping the bird. If the bird is able to fly, it usually gets tangled in branches. Many birds starve to death dangling from a tree.

Photo: Stan Ashbrook

Hooked Bird. *This brown pelican, with an open wound in its chest, was snagged by a fish hook. If not treated, birds like this often die from infected wounds.*

Photo: Stan Ashbrook

Snagged Bird. *Entangled in loose fishing line, a bird was caught in a tree and starved to death.*

The Peaceful Pelican

Pax was the first brown pelican hatched and reared in captivity by permanently crippled parents. Many *ornithologists* (scientists who study birds) and other scientists said it couldn't be done, but Pax proved them wrong.

It was a great day when the three-month-old pelican flew off to his freedom.

Photo: Stan Ashbrook

Baby Pax. *The first chick hatched by disabled brown pelican parents, Pax proved all the naysayers wrong.*

But it was a sad day a few years later when a very sick Pax returned to the Sanctuary on his own. Pax stuck his beak through slats in the gate where he had been raised. His parents were still there.

When volunteers let him in, Pax headed straight to the pen where he'd been hatched. He was identified by a band on his leg (worn by all pelicans hatched at the Sanctuary).

Rehabilitators examined Pax and found a small fishing hook stuck in his back. Later that night, the famous brown pelican died. A second hook was found puncturing his stomach wall. Like many other brown pelicans, Pax had swallowed a hook after grabbing a hooked fish.

Although Ralph grieved for the pelican, he was pleased with Pax's lifespan. The brown pelican that was hatched in spite of his parents' handicaps lived an average number of years for a wild pelican.

Recyclers of the Sky

Vinnie, a black vulture, was hungry. When his sharp eyes spotted a dead opossum along the road, he banked to the right and soared low over a highway.

A few hops later and he was feasting on the body, quickly stuffing himself. Soon he had pigged out on opossum.

When Vinnie heard the roar of a car, he jumped into the air for takeoff, but his body was too slow and heavy. The car's front fender slammed the vulture into a nearby tree.

He landed with a dull thud. Later that day, when he was able to stand, he tried to fly, but his right wing wouldn't work.

Vinnie's survival instinct told him that he'd better find cover before he became somebody's dinner. He slowly hopped into bushes and hid.

For the next week, Vinnie hobbled weakly around the bushes and slept a lot. Although the wing healed, the bones weren't lined up correctly. He could fly only in short spurts with uneven flaps.

The last time Vinnie flew wild and free, he leaped into the air, trying to gain altitude and soar with outstretched wings, as he had done so many times before. But his wing was not strong enough. He was crash-landed on grass.

Suddenly Vinnie realized that humans lived in a house on the grass. When they approached him, the black vulture hissed, swaying back and forth, warning them not to touch him.

The people notified Suncoast Seabird Sanctuary about the strange black bird. Vinnie was captured by volunteers.

Now a permanent resident at the Sanctuary, Vinnie teaches people about the important role that scavengers play in nature.

He has to put up with a lot of prejudice because people associate vultures with death, disgusting meals, and bad smells. Imagine the smells we'd have to put up with if vultures *didn't* eat dead animals.

Photo: Shannon K. Jacobs

Black Vultures. *Some people think vultures are disgusting, but others appreciate how useful — and resourceful — the birds are. (They also have some fascinating survival tricks.)*

People also think vultures are dirty, but Vinnie proves them wrong again. He can be seen bathing and preening quite often. If vultures had dirty feathers, they would never be able to get off the ground, let alone soar beyond the sky.

According to rehabilitators, vultures have some interesting survival tricks. One is to vomit on whatever frightens them or tries to take their food.

Another trick to beat the summer heat? They splatter their droppings on their legs.

No wonder vulture legs are so white in the summer!

WILD CARE, Inc.

Location:	Brewster, Massachusetts (on Cape Cod)
Description:	Home-based center; treated 1,400 native and migrating birds, mammals, and reptiles in 1996
Staff:	Director Karen Von den Deale, 30 year-round volunteers, 70-90 baby bird volunteers (May through August)
Funding:	Donations, memberships, fundraisers
Programs:	Yes
Newsletter:	*Wild Times*, published twice a year
Tours:	No

Wildlife rehabilitator Karen Von den Deale was honored with a "Hero's Award" from the *Cape Cod Times*. Bravo to the *Times* for recognizing Karen's devotion to wild creatures and her contributions to Cape Cod!

Karen founded WILD CARE in 1994. It's the only full-time, full-service rehabilitation center on Cape Cod.

In addition to treating native birds, mammals, and reptiles, Karen cares for sick and injured birds that migrate along the Atlantic Coast flyway. In one year, WILD CARE admitted 87 *different* species.

Wild Wildlife Clinic

Managing a busy wildlife clinic is a lot of work. To make the best use of her time, Karen sends baby mammals to WILD CARE's volunteers who are licensed rehabilitators in the area. (Baby mammals need to eat day *and* night, remember.)

Some of the volunteers who help out year-round never come to the center at all. They work from their homes, handling WILD CARE'S 24-hour telephone hotline. They answer calls about injured wildlife or human-wildlife conflicts.

WILD CARE receives hundreds of orphaned birds every year. To prepare for the mob, Karen trains volunteers from the community to help in the center's baby bird nursery.

During the spring and summer, 70 volunteers work in the baby bird nursery. Each volunteer works a three-hour shift once a week. Shifts start at six o'clock in the morning and end at 9 o'clock at night.

Photo: Karen Von den Deale

Early Birds. *Morning setup at WILD CARE. All dishes are labeled with the animal to be fed and the food preparation.*

"You've got to feed insect-eating birds 15-16 hours a day, or they won't live," explained Karen. "You can't just cover them up at five in the evening — they'd be dead in the morning."

"So, chickadees, nuthatches, and wrens are fed from dawn to dusk. Also, you have to make up different formulas for different species of birds. For example, finches don't eat what chickadees eat."

Photo: Karen Von den Deale

Puppet Mom. *A hand puppet, shaped like a great horned owl, is used to teach a baby owl how to eat. It helps prevent human-imprinting.*

Educational programs offered by WILD CARE have included "Our Feathered Friends," describing the history, habits, behavior, and rehabilitation of local birds; and "House on My Back," detailing life cycles and survival needs of Cape Cod turtles.

Peninsulas Are Special

Cape Cod is a *peninsula*, meaning it's bordered on three sides by water. A peninsula — which is almost an island — is special for wildlife rehabilitation. Why?

Because wildlife can't get on or off the peninsula very easily. Therefore, they can be more easily controlled.

Cape Cod is one of the few places in the U.S. that doesn't have rabies, and the people of Massachusetts want it to stay rabies-free. So wildlife officials put out food baited with rabies vaccine. When animals eat it, they become *immune to* (protected from) rabies.

"No rabies" is good news for Cape Cod rehabbers, who can treat rabies vector species, such as raccoons, skunks, bats, and foxes. They still have to be careful, though. There could always be the first case, possibly from a visiting dog or cat.

A Ghoul of a Gull

One winter was unusually cold on Cape Cod. A herring gull, found in a snowbank and brought to the Center, was one of the harsh weather's victims.

"Everybody kept saying what a nice bird it was," Karen said. "Well, you *know* you've got a sick or dead gull when it's nice to you!"

The skinny gull was so weak he couldn't stand up. Karen tube-fed the gull, treating him also for parasites, but the gull didn't improve. After three days with no progress, she decided to check the gull's blood, hoping for a diagnosis.

Karen had never had so much trouble drawing blood from a bird. When she tried to take blood from a vein in the wing, she couldn't get *any* blood. She clipped the gull's toenail (which usually causes bleeding), but no blood there, either.

Finally, a tiny bubble of blood appeared. Karen smeared it onto a slide and rushed it to her veterinarian.

The analysis of the gull's blood was shocking. The bird's white blood cells (which fight infections) were at *zero!*

Karen asked the vet what that meant. "It means you have a dead gull," the vet said, "unless we try a blood transfusion."

Although Karen had never participated in a bird blood transfusion before, she agreed. She volunteered two donors — a backyard chicken and Alby von Webb, a tame Toulouse goose. The vet told her to come back that afternoon with the gull and goose.

Alby Von Webb is a foster mother at WILD CARE. She raises orphaned wild *goslings* (goose babies). But Alby had a new job — donating blood to a grumpy gull.

Photo: Karen Von den Deale

Swapping Blood. *Rehabilitators Mary Capitummino (left, with sick gull) and Karen Von den Deale (right, holding Alby Von Webb) head for the vet's office for a blood transfusion.*

Photo: Karen Von den Deale

Alby von Webb and Brood. *"Alby teaches the babies how to chase the volunteers, so they'll learn not to tolerate people," Karen said. "When the babies are released, they're definitely wild birds."*

That afternoon, Karen took the goose and gull to the vet's office. The vet drew some of Alby's blood and injected it into the gull.

By evening, the gull was *preening* (combing and cleaning feathers). He finally had an appetite, so Karen fed him liquid fish, and eventually, whole fish and clams.

Over the next week, the bird got better. When the vet checked the gull's blood, she found it had improved dramatically.

Karen is preparing to release the bird after he strengthens his wings for flying. Because the gull received blood from a goose, Karen gave him a fitting name — *Gooul.*

Bungee Crow

Crows are curious because they're smart birds. But sometimes, that curiosity gets them in trouble.

When a young crow sitting in a pine tree spotted a piece of loose fishing line, he leaped into the air, flapped his glossy wings, and landed next to it.

The crow pecked at the line, but it didn't move. A breeze blew the fishing line, and it wound around the crow's leg like a boa constrictor.

Disappointed that it wasn't food, the bird hopped into the air for take off. The line trailed after him.

All day the bird skipped around the grass, pecking at food containers people had dropped. When he flew into a nearby tree, the free end of the fishing line wrapped around a branch.

Later, planning to raid an overturned garbage can, the crow jumped into the air. He rose only a foot from the tree limb before he was jerked back by the line and slung upside down.

The crow was strong. He flapped his wings until he could reach a branch with his beak and free foot to pull himself upright. He pecked at the line that had tightened around his foot, but it didn't budge.

For several hours, the crow leaped into the air, was snapped back, and dangled. Then he flapped himself back up to the branch, only to do it all over again.

By the end of the first day, the line had become tangled in his wing. By the second day, the weak crow was close to death. Still, he tried to get free.

People on the ground had watched the crow frantically trying to free himself in the tall pine tree. When they realized he couldn't get loose, they called WILD CARE. A very brave volunteer climbed the tree and rescued the dying crow.

The bird truly was on his last leg when brought to the center. Karen cut off the fishing line, cleaned up his leg wound, and let him rest. When he was strong enough to eat, she fed him.

It took awhile, but the crow's wing healed well, and the bird was released. Curiosity cost the crow a serious injury. Maybe it also taught him a valuable lesson in survival.

Photo: Karen Von den Deale

Curious Crow. *After its rescue, the crow did well. It was released back to the wild.*

BIRDS OF PREY FOUNDATION

Location:	Broomfield, Colorado
Description:	Large center treating more than 400 birds of prey yearly
Staff:	Two full-time, one part-time staff; more than 50 volunteers
Funding:	Donations, memberships, fundraisers, weekly bingo
Newsletter:	Annual Christmas letter describing year's events and birds
Programs:	School and community visits with education birds
Tours:	No; annual open house for members and sponsors

Sigrid began rehabilitating raptors 15 years ago, starting in her backyard. At first, she learned from a very skilled wildlife veterinarian.

Then she continued educating herself, studying and collecting books on raptors, and taking courses on wildlife rehabilitation.

When she gives programs at schools and communities, Sigrid likes to weave the natural history of birds into true stories.

"I love having eye contact with a child with questions," Sigrid said. "I love, too, the shadow programs, where a child comes to stay a day or a number of hours, following us around."

"A true healer" is how Sigrid Ueblacker is described. She is founder and director of Birds of Prey Foundation (BOP).

Sigrid admits that she's always loved animals. "When I was a little girl in Austria," she said, "I didn't want to read until someone gave me a book about animals."

Sigrid is known for her high professional standards as well as compassionate care. She has created a rehabilitation center admired by many. Birds of Prey is not open to the public, but Sigrid occasionally schedules tours. People from several countries have visited the center.

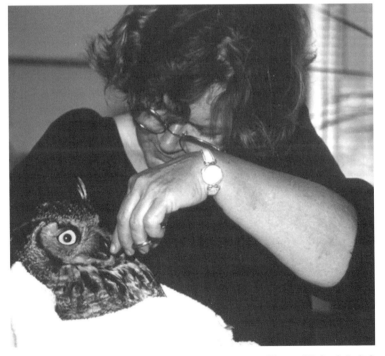

Photo: Michael Judish

A True Healer. *Sigrid Ueblacker uses forceps to feed a great horned owl that was injured when caught in a leg hold trap.*

Roomy Flight Cages

Twenty-nine large flight cages at Birds of Prey Foundation are temporary homes for bald and golden eagles, falcons, hawks, and owls.

The pleasant, sunny enclosures are filled with branches, ladders for climbing, trees, grass, and large pools for drinking and bathing.

Photo: Dave Felder

Hawk Cage. *Birds of Prey Foundation has some of the largest raptor rehabilitation enclosures anywhere, allowing birds to exercise whenever they want.*

Because they are in such huge enclosures, birds are able to fly on their own, anytime they want. This gives them a lot of freedom to practice flying.

Birds of Prey Foundation rehabilitates about 400 birds of prey each year. Volunteers donate thousands of hours rescuing and rehabilitating the birds.

They also do fundraisers, clean cages, and raise live food sources — rabbits, quail, and mice.

Human Therapy

Humans sometimes get rehabilitated at the Foundation, too. People who need to work off traffic violations by performing community service apply at the center. A carefully selected few work about 4,000 hours a year.

These volunteers help with cleaning, building, and animal care. In fact, most of the Foundation's intensive care unit was built through community service.

Few community volunteers leave the Foundation without being touched by their experience.

One man who had to work off 100 hours was given the job of cleaning the rabbit hut. Within a month, he'd named all the rabbits.

"His probation officer wanted to know what we did to him because the man's attitude had changed so much," Sigrid said. "The man used to complain all the time about his life. Suddenly he was announcing, 'At lunch today I saw a Swainson's hawk!'"

Photo: Trish Phillips

Hamlet *suffered from lead poisoning.*

To Be or Not to Be — Free

Hamlet, a bald eagle, was very sick from lead poisoning when admitted to Birds of Prey. He probably had eaten an animal injured or killed with lead shot.

Hungry raptors occasionally feed on roadkill or other *carrion* (dead animals). They also are poisoned by lead pellets, lead sinkers, or poisons intentionally put out to kill wild creatures.

BOP's veterinarian, Dr. Lee Eggleston, treated Hamlet for the lead poisoning. Sigrid credits the veterinarian with saving the eagle's life.

Because Hamlet acted depressed and wouldn't eat on his own, Sigrid stayed with him over Christmas, putting off her family celebration.

After many weeks of rollercoasting health, Hamlet began to improve. Soon he was moved into a flight cage to practice his flying skills with other recovering eagles. At that point Sigrid stopped handling him.

"It was time to let go," she wrote in her newsletter. "This is the objective of our efforts: to care and to nurse when our wild birds need our help so desperately, and then to stand back quietly, watch their progress, and eventually return them to the homeland when they are ready to fend for themselves."

One warm, sunny day in December, 350 people gathered for the release of four bald eagles that had been rehabilitated at Birds of Prey Foundation. Hamlet was one of them.

After a blessing ceremony given by a Native American medicine man, the four birds were set free to walk the wild winds.

Beautiful Blue Lady

Blue Lady, an endangered peregrine falcon, hadn't healed well at another rehabilitation center, so she was sent to Birds of Prey Foundation. Pneumonia had damaged the falcon's lungs, and her left wing drooped from an old fracture.

No injured peregrine falcon had been returned to the wilds of Colorado in 15 years. Would Blue Lady make it?

Sigrid gave her the best opportunity to heal. She placed Blue Lady in a large flight cage, reduced human contact, and fed her good falcon food.

Blue Lady. *Would this beautiful, endangered bird make it?*

Photo: Sigrid Ueblacker

In response, Blue Lady practiced flying across the cage several times a day, strengthening her wings. To Sigrid's delight, Blue Lady's wing soon straightened out.

In September, Sigrid caught the falcon and put a band on her leg. That meant that Blue Lady would be released. Each band has a specific number on it.

Sigrid and Blue Lady traveled to the release site in a plane, flying together over the Rocky Mountains.

Then they journeyed by car to the Colorado National Monument. That's where the injured bird had been found eight months before. Above a deep canyon, Sigrid released the beautiful Blue Lady.

"She left my hands and disappeared below the rim of the canyon," Sigrid described in her newsletter. "She turned into a ghostly blue shadow and became the hunter she once used to be. She cruised along the canyon walls as she flew from sunshine into shade."

Over the next few weeks, four sightings of her were reported. Thanks to Birds of Prey Foundation, Blue Lady once again graced the canyons.

Blue Lady has made her home 100 miles from the release site, where she has raised several nests of young.

Photo: Wendy Shattil and Bob Rozinski

Canyon Cruisers. A healed Blue Lady watches over her young.

Becoming Champions
of the Wild

Photo: Critter Alley

Wild Again. *A curious raccoon pauses to pose after release.*

Chapter 17

Protecting Wildlife

Wildlife rehabilitators recommend the following 12 steps everyone can take to protect wildlife.

1. TAKE RESPONSIBILITY FOR PETS

At least 50 million cats run loose in our towns, cities, and countrysides. If only 10% of these cats kill one bird a day, that still adds up to *hundreds of millions* of birds that die every year because of loose cats. They also kill more than a billion small mammals and reptiles a year.

Photo: Greenwood Wildlife Sanctuary

Feline Killers.

> **Cat attacks are the most preventable of all bird injuries and deaths.**

How can responsible owners protect birds and small mammals? Keep cats inside. People do it all the time, and pets adjust.

First, the cat should be neutered or spayed to reduce its urge to roam. Next, slowly cut back on the time the cat stays outside at night, until it's not going out at all. It takes time, but cats (and people) can change.

Your inside cat won't be carrying pollen, dirt, and other worrisome things indoors. Also, your cat will have more energy, since it won't be out stalking the streets at night.

But the best part is the extra time you'll have with your cat. The average lifespan of a housecat is 18 years.

Outdoor cats live an average of only five years because of car hits, dog attacks, and diseases.

For specific information on how to make your outdoor cat a happy indoor cat, contact:
Linda Winter
American Bird Conservancy
Cats Indoors! Campaign
1250 24th St. NW, Suite 400
Washington, DC 20037
(202) 778-9619
email: LWINTER@ABCBIRDS.ORG

Loose Dogs

When owners let their dogs run loose in city parks, open spaces, or wilderness areas, the dogs chase and kill wildlife. Young animals, especially, are hurt.

Some dogs hang out in hunting packs. If their owners aren't careful about keeping them in a yard or house at night, dogs sneak off and join canine packs. These packs terrorize and kill wild creatures, even those in zoos.

We can't blame dogs or cats for the hundreds of millions of wild animals they kill every year. Only owners, who are responsible for their pets, can stop this assault on wildlife.

2. RESPECT WILDLIFE HABITAT

Are you aware of wild creatures when you hike or bike in the mountains, boat on a lake, or snowmobile in a forest? Do you think about their need for privacy and quiet? Just as we need to feel safe and secure in our homes, so wild creatures need peace and quiet.

Without the four walls of a house to protect them, wild animals depend on human consideration.

Protect Nests

Being respectful of wildlife is especially important during nesting times. If adults raising their young are frightened off by loud or destructive human activity, they may become separated from their babies and abandon them.

Stay on trails, so wildlife have areas to themselves. When you see nests, keep a respectful distance away. Don't get too close to adults with their young.

3. HUNT AND SHOOT RESPONSIBLY

Hunters play important roles in protecting wild animals and habitats. Responsible hunters don't kill animals they don't plan to eat, and they don't shoot wildlife for target practice.

Unfortunately, some irresponsible people have guns, and they shoot at anything that moves. Gunshot is still a major source of injuries for bald eagles and other raptors.

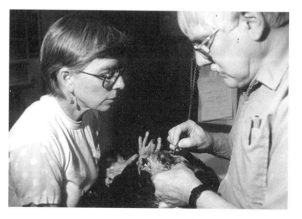

Photo: B.D. Wehrfritz

Shot Out of the Sky. *Rehabilitator Susan Ahalt and Dr. Malcolm Blessing examine Memory, a bald eagle shot by a high powered rifle. She survived but can't be released because of the injury.*

The education eagle that Diana Shaffer (Wildlife Resqu Haus in Yorktown, Indiana) takes into classrooms lost a wing because someone filled it with buckshot. Diana reminds students what happens when someone carelessly shoots a wild creature.

"How would you like to spend your life in your room, not ever able to go out and play, ride on your bike with friends, or watch TV?" she asks. "This eagle has to spend the rest of her life in a cage because someone shot her for fun."

Prevent Lead Poisoning

Responsible hunters don't use lead shot. It was banned in the U.S. because it causes lead poisoning.

Many birds of prey are poisoned by lead because they eat animals that have been killed with lead shot. This often happens when the raptors are migrating and very hungry. Lead poisoning is fatal if not treated quickly.

Responsible hunters also report poachers (and others who destroy wildlife and habitat) to their state wildlife department or to a wildlife rehabilitator. That keeps spoilers from ruining the natural world for everyone else.

4. FISH RESPONSIBLY

Lead fishing sinkers cause lead poisoning when water birds eat them. Responsible fishermen don't use lead sinkers. There are other choices — steel and nontoxic sinkers.

Fishing Hooks and Lines

Fishing line is a major source of injury and death for *threatened* (could become endangered) brown pelicans, as well as other water birds.

Responsible fishermen don't leave loose fishing line in lakes or oceans. They remove the line and dispose of it properly. Responsible fishermen don't cut the line if a bird gets hooked, because the bird will become entangled in trees or bushes and starve, unable to get loose.

There are other choices of fishing line besides monofilament. Some are made from cotton or other biodegradable fibers.

Photo: Karen Von den Deale

Hooked Gull. *Fishermen can prevent hook injuries.*

Preventing Hooking Injuries

- Before casting, make sure no water birds are flying above.
- If water birds are close by, wait a few minutes, until they leave the area.
- Don't pull in a fish on a hook close to a bird; the bird will gobble it up.
- Never leave baited fishing tackle out in the open, unattended.
- Don't leave hooks hanging from the end of exposed fishing rods.
- Don't throw used fishing line or other plastic into the water.
- Don't feed water birds where people are fishing.

Adapted with permission from Suncoast Seabird Sanctuary

5. BOAT RESPONSIBLY

Responsible boaters, water skiers, and jet skiers constantly look out for water birds, nesting birds, manatees, dolphins, and other water creatures. If any are spotted, they slow down and stay a respectful distance away.

Responsible boaters stay away from marshy areas, where birds nest or hide. They also don't boat too close to islands or speed around places where birds nest. Waves can drown young birds and drive off parents.

6. DRIVE RESPONSIBLY

It takes a lot of time for big birds to get into the air. Responsible car drivers slow down in places where large birds hang out. These include bridges and causeways. Drivers should also reduce speed when spotting a large bird on the side of the road. It's probably eating roadkill.

If birds see cars coming, they'll fly toward an open area. Usually, that's the middle of the road. When you see a bird alongside the road, give it time to take off, or you'll hit it.

Many mammals are blinded by headlights. They're often hit by cars when crossing roads, because they freeze when caught in car lights. Responsible drivers slow down in areas where these animals frequently cross.

Driving snowmobiles or motorcycles into wildlife habitat also requires attention. Stay on trails. Don't bother or chase wildlife.

7. CLEAN UP LITTER AND POLLUTION

In 1995, *four million pieces of garbage, weighing 2.5 million pounds,* were picked up along U.S. coastal shores. Think how much is not collected but ends up floating in the ocean or sinking to the bottom.

The number one coastal problem was filtered cigarette butts. Also, hundreds of thousands of plastic cups, lids, food bags, straws, bottles, and wrappers were picked up along beaches.

Trash looks like food to wild animals. They eat it and feed it to their young. Plastic bags look like jellyfish, which is a sea turtle delicacy. Many dead sea turtles have starved to death, their intestines filled with plastic.

Deadly Balloons

Sick, stranded marine mammals have been found with plastic bags and balloons clogging their stomachs.

Helium balloons can travel far when released, and they end up on land and in the sea. For this reason, some states have banned the release of helium balloons.

People can still enjoy helium balloons without endangering wildlife. One way is to use ceiling bags to catch the balloons after they're released.

Another choice is to rent homing pigeons and release them all at once. It's more dramatic and safer for wildlife.

Plastic Rings

If six-pack or four-pack plastic rings or other plastic items aren't cut up before being recycled or thrown away, they can become deadly chokers for wild animals.

Every year, rehabilitators admit ducks, raccoons, squirrels, seals, and opossums, among many others, that are trapped in plastic rings. Often the animals can't be caught. Most starve to death, because the tight rings prevent them from swallowing.

Deadly Chokers. *Cut up plastic sunglasses, 4-pack and 6-pack rings, bottle rings, and other plastic garbage before throwing away or recyling. They can be deadly for wildlife.*

Photo: Critter Alley

8. THINK BEFORE FEEDING WILDLIFE

Feeding wild animals by hand is one of the worst things you can do. Why? It makes wildlife too trusting of people. Then they expect food from everyone.

Photo: Shannon K. Jacobs

Don't Hand-Feed Wildlife. *It's dangerous for you and for the animals, especially if they learn to trust*

Many people are afraid of wild creatures, and they become more frightened when approached by friendly wildlife. What do you think will happen to these animals?

Hand-feeding wild animals is dangerous for people, too. Wildlife are unpredictable. If you give peanuts to a squirrel, it might be fine one day. The next day it might jump on you or chomp on a finger with chisel-sharp teeth.

Attracting Crowds

Some people put out food for wildlife, thinking they're doing them a favor. But the food ends up attracting large numbers of critters, and that's dangerous for everyone.

The more dense the wildlife populations are, the more risk there is for disease. Animals also fight more when crowded together, especially if food supplies dwindle or are stopped.

When people stop feeding wild animals, some animals go hungry. Out of desperation, they may raid gardens, farms, or homes, and become dangerous. Then angry people demand that the animals be removed or killed.

Photo: Paula Stolebarger

Open Pits. *This young raccoon, attracted to a dumpster full of food, became trapped inside. The quick-thinking photographer placed a board inside, enabling the wayward coon to climb out.*

Photo: Urban Wildlife Rescue

Chomper. *Hand-fed regularly in a city park, Chomper bit 12 people before he was caught, rehabilitated, and released far away from people.*

A Fed Fox is a Dead Fox

In Kansas, a man fed a fox every day for months. He taught the creature to scratch at his back door for food. Then the man went away on a trip, leaving the fox without a food source. The hungry fox ran all over the neighborhood, scratching on back doors, looking for food.

When a frightened woman saw the fox at her back door, she thought it had rabies because it wasn't afraid of people. She called the state wildlife agency, and someone came out and shot the fox.

The fox was tested and found not to have rabies. It was just a healthy, dead fox that was too trusting of people.

9. DON'T KIDNAP WILDLIFE

Wild animals belong in the wild. Captive creatures yearn for their freedom, and they never get over it. It's wrong to cage these free spirits.

Wildlife Diseases

It's dangerous to keep wild animals in your home. Many carry *zoonoses*. These are diseases that can be passed from wildlife to humans.

Although wildlife rehabilitators know how to avoid getting zoonoses, the average person does not. Some zoonotic diseases can be fatal.

In one nonfatal case, a woman picked up a young fox and took it home as a "pet." The fox played with the kids, cats, and dog. It hopped on the furniture and slept on the beds.

But when the fox got sick and began losing its hair, the woman got worried. She took the animal to Operation WildLife in Linwood, Kansas.

While examining the fox, wildlife rehabilitator Diane Johnson noticed that the woman kept scratching herself. Hunks of hair fell out when the woman scratched her head. Diane scraped some of the fox's skin and hair and looked at it under the microscope.

"This fox has mange," Diane told the woman. "And so do you."

Mange is a skin disease caused by tiny *mites* (parasites) that burrow under the skin. It often causes hair loss and can make animals sick enough to die.

Although it's easily cured in humans, people can suffer from itching and hair loss. The fox had run all over the woman's house, infecting people and pets with mites. After leaving the fox with the rehabilitator, the woman and her family had to throw away their rugs, bedding, curtains, and carpeting.

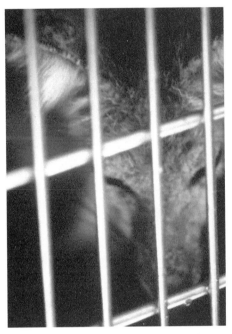

Photo: Diane Johnson

Mange. This young fox with mange infected a house when he was brought home as a "pet."

Wild Behaviors

Wild animals also have wild *instincts* (behaviors they're born with) and learned wild behaviors. One man's ignorance about this almost cost him dearly.

When the man found a young coyote pup near its dead, car-hit mother, he took the coyote home. He thought it would be fun to have a pet coyote.

Would you expect a wild coyote to act like a tame, domestic dog? This man did.

He fenced off the kitchen area for the pup. That became its territory — where it ate and slept.

The man's three-year-old son loved to watch the pup. One day, the little boy climbed over the gate to pet the "doggie" while the coyote was eating. The boy didn't mean to, but he threatened the pup.

Photo: Diane Johnson

Dangerous Pets. *A coyote pup, taken home as a "pet," nearly attacked a man's young son.*

Acting on instinct to protect its food and territory, the coyote lunged at the boy. The father grabbed his son just in time, saving him from being attacked.

Was it the coyote's fault for behaving like the animal it was? The man finally admitted that he'd made a mistake by taking a wild animal into his home. He took the pup to Diane Johnson at Operation WildLife in Linwood, Kansas.

Diane taught the coyote how to be properly wild. It was released later.

10. DON'T BUY EXOTIC PETS

With permits in certain states, it's legal to capture animals from the wild, breed them, and sell their young. Does being legal make it right?

Wild animals never make good pets, even if born in captivity. All wild creatures have instincts they have no control over.

Photo: Shannon K. Jacobs

Sad Wild "Pet" Story. *A woman had this cougar declawed as a kitten. But she had no decent place to keep him, so wildlife officials took the cat away from her. If a wildlife rehabilitator couple had not taken the cat, he would have been euthanized. The couple is now responsible for the care of this magnificent animal that will spend the rest of his life caged.*

As they get older, wild animals are driven by instinct to find a mate, protect their territory, food, and young, and stay alive. When they reach full size, these animals become uncontrollable, unpredictable, and dangerous.

What do people do with wild "pets" when the cute babies grow into snarling adults?

Usually they lock them in cages or basements or turn them loose in the wild, unprepared to survive on their own.

Sometimes, people sell captive wild animals to game ranches. These places charge people to shoot the helpless animals for "sport."

Wouldn't it be better to prevent such horrors and not make wild animals "pets" in the first place? Wild critters don't ever become "tame," no matter how affectionate they are when they're young.

Wild animals' survival instincts tell them to fear and avoid humans. But if they're raised by people, they learn to trust us. This really confuses them, and their behavior becomes even more unpredictable.

The best pets for families are *domestic* (bred to be tame) animals such as cats, dogs, hamsters, gerbils, and rabbits.

Do you know how long it took to *domesticate* (tame) wolves into the dogs we know today? At least tens of thousands of years.

Cats have been domesticated for only a few thousand years. Can you tell? Do cats seem wilder than dogs, with stronger instincts?

If you buy wild animals, you're encouraging people to steal them from the wild. These animals often live in cruel conditions. Many never live long enough to be sold.

For each animal that's bought, there are thousands more that die from injuries, diseases, starvation, and the stress of being crammed into tiny, airless containers when they're used to being free.

Would you really want a wild "pet," knowing how dangerous, expensive, and miserable it would become?

Photo: Shannon K. Jacobs

Stolen. *This prairie dog was dug up in Texas and sold to a pet store in Florida. If people stopped buying wild animals, this wouldn't happen.*

167

11. Make Your Yard Wildlife Friendly

Pesticides are designed to kill. They rarely kill just insects.

Wildlife rehabilitator Elaine Thrune (Wild Again in St. Cloud, Minnesota) described a situation she's experienced several times:

A woman and her daughter bring in a sick bird. The little girl carries the bird in her hand. When she opens her fingers, the bird flips onto its back and twitches all over. It's eyelids flutter violently.

Elaine has seen this happen with other sick birds. She knows what it is.

"Has anyone sprayed their lawn with pesticides in your neighborhood in the last few days?" Elaine asks.

The woman answers, "We had someone spray our lawn yesterday."

Elaine explains that the bird is acting as though it's poisoned by pesticide spray.

"We did this?" the woman cries. "But the man who sprayed said it was perfectly safe. He didn't even wear boots when he sprayed."

Elaine suggests that the woman use nontoxic sprays on her lawn if she wants to stop poisoning birds. The woman shakes her head.

"I don't mind a few dandelions," she says, "but my husband insists on a perfect lawn."

Pesticides Kill

Pesticides kill insects. But what eats the poisoned insects? Birds.

Photo: Critter Alley

Pesticide Deformity. *A young robin has a deformed beak because its mother was exposed to pesticides.*

What eats birds poisoned by pesticides? Foxes, raptors, opossums, raccoons, snakes, hawks. Sometimes, cats and dogs eat them, too.

Pesticides seep into our water supplies, rivers, and lakes. Who drinks the water?

Nontoxic Choices

There are many nonpoisonous products available. You can check with experts at garden supply centers, botanical gardens, or wild bird centers.

They'll give you good advice about how to improve yards without poisoning all life forms.

If your family uses a lawn service, ask the company for a list of your lawn problems and the chemicals being used to treat them. *Always insist on using the least toxic chemicals.*

If you had the choice to give up 10% of your lawn and garden to insects and other hungry critters — in exchange for healthy yards, water, wildlife, and people — what would you choose?

Planting for Wildlife

Did you know that hummingbirds and butterflies like certain plants? That specific trees are great for birds to nest in? That you can build homes for bats?

Planting and creating homes for wildlife help replace wild foods and shelters that are destroyed by development. They provide wild creatures with food, water, cover, and places to raise their young.

This is a more natural and effective way to provide food for wildlife, rather than putting out food or hand-feeding them.

If you'd like to learn more about planting for wildlife, look through books and videos in libraries, bookstores, and nature centers. Also, contact the National Wildlife Federation's Backyard Wildlife Habitat Program (www.nwf.org/habitats).

For 26 years NWF has sponsored a Backyard Wildlife Habitat program. National certificates have been given to 20,000 projects around the world, including homes, schools, and businesses.

Photo: Shannon K. Jacobs

Hummingbird Garden. *Fourth-grader John Weege in Littleton, Colorado, enjoys gardening for hummingbirds and butterflies, because he gets to see them, identify them, and learn about them.*

Careful Mowing

It's a good idea to check your yard before mowing the grass. Some birds nest on the ground. A few mammals nest in the grass, even near houses.

Walk around the area and peek into the high grass. If you find a nest of rabbits or ground-nesting birds, consider waiting one or two weeks to mow, until they're gone. If you can't wait, call a wildlife rehabilitator and ask for advice.

169

Careful Tree Trimming

Unfortunately most people and tree companies trim trees in the springtime, right at the beginning of nesting season.

Many baby birds and squirrels become orphaned or injured when trees are trimmed. Ask your family to check tree branches before trimming. If nests with babies in them are found, call a wildlife rehabilitator before moving the nests.

You also can help by banging on the tree a couple of times a day for a few days before the tree is trimmed or cut. That warns mother squirrels and raccoons to move their babies from the tree. For squirrels, this should be done in spring and fall. They give birth during both seasons.

12. PREVENT WINDOW COLLISIONS

It's estimated that 95 millions birds are killed each year from hitting home or office windows.

Why do birds smash into windows like kamikaze pilots? Because windows reflect trees and sky, which is where the birds need to fly to escape cats or raptors.

People have tried several ways to avoid bird and window collisions. Some put silhouettes of hawks on their windows or hang up wind socks or wind chimes. Tape or ribbons on windows may work, too.

One of the big problems is that bird feeders, which attract birds, often are placed near windows so people can enjoy the birds.

When birds are scared by loud noises or the shadow of a real hawk, they don't have a good escape route.

If you are having problems with birds hitting your windows, try putting up hawk silhouettes, ribbons, or wind socks.

You might also experiment with placing feeders in different places, either very close to or very far from windows.

If feeders are placed about a foot away from windows, birds may not be able to gain enough takeoff speed to hurt themselves.

Feeders hung in open areas, farther away from windows, allow birds to take off in all directions.

Photo: Shannon K. Jacobs

Feeding Fledgling. *If birds are hitting your windows, try moving feeders closer to or farther away from the house.*

170

Chapter 18

Wildproofing Your Home

Some people think that the best way to handle an unwanted animal in the house or yard is to kill it. But that doesn't solve the problem.

Find out what is attracting animals to your home. Is it food? Water? Shelter?

> The best way to get rid of unwanted wild animals: Get rid of what attracts them.

Photo: *Urban Wildlife Rescue*

For the Birds? *Bird food attracts other critters, too.*

WILD-PROOFING TIPS

1. Take pet food inside at night. Remove the invitation to unwanted visitors.

2. Put out enough birdseed for just one day. This discourages nocturnal prowlers — such as raccoons, skunks, and opossums — from raiding your bird feeder.

3. Store garbage in cans with tight lids. Don't use just bags. If possible, keep trash in a closed garage or shed until collection day.

4. Seal up cracks and holes in your house. Use heavy mesh wire to close up entry holes in the foundation, eaves, attic, chimney, or under porches. First, make sure no animals (including birds) are trapped inside.

5. Cover your chimney with a cap. Measure the chimney opening, take the measurements to your local hardware store, and ask for a chimney cap. Before installing the cap, make sure no animals (including birds) are trapped inside.

ENCOURAGING ANIMALS TO LEAVE

If you have an unwanted animal resident, call a wildlife rehabilitator before you trap, poison, kill, or chase off the creature. Rehabilitators will give you sound advice on what to do and how to do it humanely.

During the spring, many animals seek dark, quiet shelters where they can give birth and raise young.

If an animal family is nesting in your house, try being patient for a few weeks. That's usually all it takes for the babies to be weaned. Then there are many more choices for you and the furry family.

If the mother is chased off, trapped, or removed, the babies will starve.

Getting Rid of What Animals Like

The best way to evict wild creatures is to get rid of what they like — dark and quiet. Leaving a light on in an attic, chimney, or under a porch sometimes can be enough to discourage the family.

Radios tuned into talk shows and turned up loud will drive off some creatures. Animals may get used to music (even rock music), but they don't like human voices.

Stinky smells, such as rags soaked in ammonia and placed in the sleeping area, can send wild creatures running off.

Wait until the babies are gone before you use any chemicals, though. Never use poisons or harmful chemicals. Who knows where they'll end up? It might be in your cat or dog's stomach.

Mix up the methods you use — stinky smell, light, noise.

That's so the animals don't get too used to any one method. They are, after all, very adaptable.

Beware of Protective Mothers

Be very careful of mothers with young. Never get between mothers and their babies. Most mothers will attack if they think their young are threatened.

Photo: *Urban Wildlife Rescue*

Fighter Moms. *Don't get between a mother and her young. She may attack.*

Chapter 19

What Can Kids Do?

NAMING NATURE

Kids have always had a special relationship with animals. Because of this, you can do a lot to help wildlife.

First, ask yourself what you know about your wild neighbors. Can you name two mammals, two reptiles, and two birds living near you? It's much easier to care about something when you know its name.

Do you have a favorite native animal? Where does it live? What does it eat? Draw or photograph the animal, or write a poem about it. Learn all you can about the animal and its habitat, then work hard to protect both.

Share your knowledge with friends and family. All wild creatures, like all people, are fascinating. They can teach us amazing things. They deserve our attention and admiration.

Learning About Nature

Learning about nature means spending as much time as possible outdoors. You don't have to go far away to enjoy nature.

Photo: *Shannon K. Jacobs*

Tracking Tadpoles. *For 9-year-old Miquette Reardon, it's challenging and fun to catch and release tadpoles.*

173

Nature is a spider spinning a web in a corner of your porch.

Nature is a red-tailed hawk perched on a
    telephone pole, watching for prey.
Nature is a fox squirrel burying nuts in
    a city park.
Nature is a park, lake, or trees along
    city streets.
Nature is the desert, beach, or mountains.
Nature is your back yard.

PRACTICING THE "THREE Ls"

Dr. John Huckabee (director and staff veterinarian for Wildlife Center of Harris County Precinct 4 in Tomball, Texas) recommended three important ways to learn about wildlife. He called them "The Three L's" — look, learn, and leave alone.

"*Look* at animals and enjoy them, but from a distance," he suggested. "*Learn* all you can about wildlife from books, magazines, television programs, videos, teachers, rehabilitators, or nature centers."

Dr. Huckabee added, "To *leave alone* means not to interfere with wildlife. Don't keep peeking into a bird's nest to see when the eggs will hatch. Don't take the nest home to see the eggs hatch."

WATCHING FEATHERED FRIENDS

Can you name two birds that live in your neighborhood all year long? What about the names of two birds that migrate through your state?

There are 780 species of birds in North America. We are very lucky to have such a variety of feathered friends.

Photo: Shannon K. Jacobs

Never Too Young. *A Colorado Bird Observatory (CBO) volunteer shows 4-year-old Erin Weber and Kyle, her younger brother, a banded migratory bird just before it's released. Groups like CBO are great ways to learn about birds and other wildlife.*

Becoming a bird watcher, or birder, is one of the easiest ways to begin learning about wildlife. Birds live everywhere.

Start by noticing the birds around your home. Listen to them. Spend a few minutes walking around your neighborhood or a nearby park, watching birds.

Even common birds like robins and crows are fun to observe. Notice their colors, their body size, the way they fly, walk, or hop. Listen to their many different songs.

Wildlife Groups

Join the Audubon Society, Sierra Club, National Wildlife Federation, or check out other groups that offer field trips and classes. There are many offered through wild bird stores, such as Wild Bird Centers and Wild Birds Unlimited.

Also, natural history museums, botanical gardens, nature centers, and state parks provide classes and field trips. These are good places to meet other people who also love to learn about wildlife.

Photo: Shannon K. Jacobs

Bird Watchers. *Binoculars help these young bird watchers identify common and rare birds that visit this city park. Have you ever counted how many species you can identify in a nearby park or neighborhood? See the bird flying in front of the girls? The bird's baby, on the next page, is hidden among cattails.*

Photo: Shannon K. Jacobs

Baby Blackbird. *A fledgling red-winged blackbird hides among cattails, waiting to be fed by its parents.*

Bird Books

When you begin to see differences in birds, you'll be ready for a bird book. There are many kids' birding guides available. Check your library, local book stores, or bird centers. If you continue with your birding interest, you might want to save up for (or ask for as a gift) binoculars to watch birds farther away.

Soon you'll become an expert on birds. You can easily show off your knowledge, because most people can't identify birds very well. For example, while walking home from school, you might point out a winged wonder in the sky and casually say to friends, "Oh, look, a Swainson's hawk."

While everyone is gawking at the sky with open mouths, not seeing a thing, you calmly point to the black speck in the sky.

"Oh, my mistake," you modestly say. "It's a black vulture riding afternoon thermals, scouting for roadkill."

Learning is Caring

Kids can do a lot to help wild creatures. Learning about your own native birds, reptiles, and mammals is an important first step. What you learn about, you'll care about. What you care about, you'll want to protect.

Photo: Cindy Rork

Learning is Caring. *Fifth-grader Andrew Rork releases two garter snakes close to where he'd caught them. "They'll do better in the wild than in a cage in my house," Andrew explained. "They were refusing to eat, and the cage was too small for them."*

176

Photo: Greg Ewert

Nature Explorers. *Youngsters living on Lopez Island, Washington, visit a local beach and find — what — a huge octopus? Nope, just harmless kelp. The island adventurers are (left to right): Hillary Zoerb (11), Emma Ewert (8), Tasha Wilson (10), Arielle Wilson (7), Laurel Horn (12), Lilly Ewert (5), and Clara Ewert (2).*

If You Find Orphaned or Injured Animals

In Good Hands. *A young burrowing owl will get proper care at Birds of Prey Foundation.*

179

Chapter 20

I Found a Baby Bird ... *Now What?*

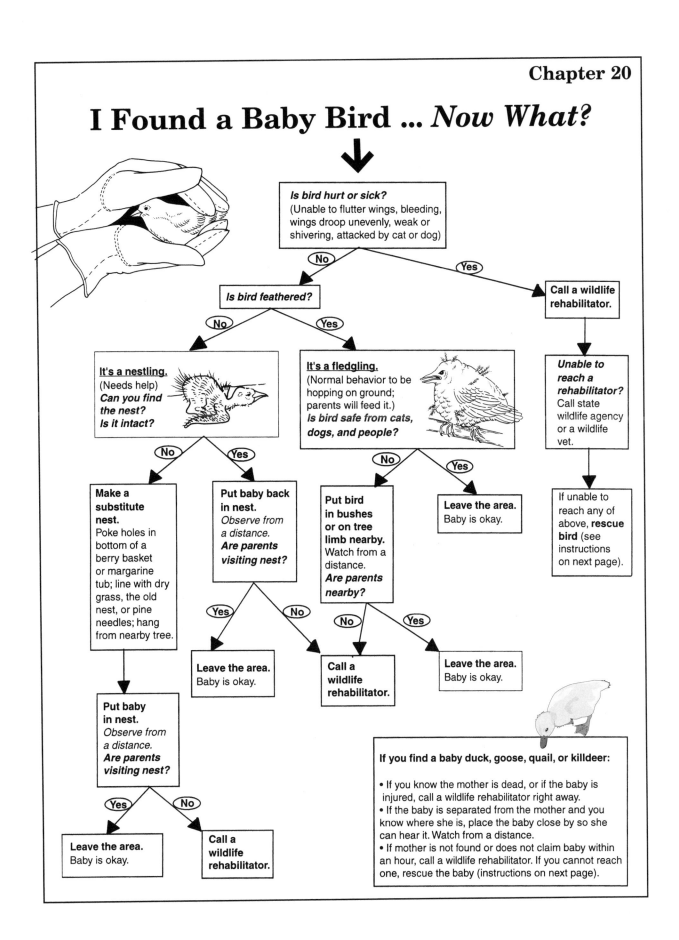

Is bird hurt or sick?
(Unable to flutter wings, bleeding, wings droop unevenly, weak or shivering, attacked by cat or dog)

No → / Yes →

Is bird feathered?

No / Yes

Call a wildlife rehabilitator.

Unable to reach a rehabilitator? Call state wildlife agency or a wildlife vet.

If unable to reach any of above, **rescue bird** (see instructions on next page).

It's a nestling.
(Needs help)
Can you find the nest?
Is it intact?

No / Yes

It's a fledgling.
(Normal behavior to be hopping on ground; parents will feed it.)
Is bird safe from cats, dogs, and people?

No / Yes

Make a substitute nest.
Poke holes in bottom of a berry basket or margarine tub; line with dry grass, the old nest, or pine needles; hang from nearby tree.

Put baby back in nest.
Observe from a distance.
Are parents visiting nest?

Yes / No

Put bird in bushes or on tree limb nearby.
Watch from a distance.
Are parents nearby?

No / Yes

Leave the area.
Baby is okay.

Put baby in nest.
Observe from a distance.
Are parents visiting nest?

Yes / No

Leave the area.
Baby is okay.

Call a wildlife rehabilitator.

Leave the area.
Baby is okay.

Leave the area.
Baby is okay.

Call a wildlife rehabilitator.

If you find a baby duck, goose, quail, or killdeer:

• If you know the mother is dead, or if the baby is injured, call a wildlife rehabilitator right away.
• If the baby is separated from the mother and you know where she is, place the baby close by so she can hear it. Watch from a distance.
• If mother is not found or does not claim baby within an hour, call a wildlife rehabilitator. If you cannot reach one, rescue the baby (instructions on next page).

How to Rescue Baby Birds

(Only adults should rescue baby birds. Before rescuing adult birds, seek guidance from a wildlife rehabilitator.)

1. **Prepare a container.** Place a clean, soft cloth with no strings or loops on the bottom of a cardboard box or cat/dog carrier with a lid. If it doesn't have air holes, make some. For smaller birds, you can use a paper sack with air holes.
2. **Protect yourself.** Wear gloves, if possible. Some birds may stab with their beaks, slice with their *talons* (claws) and slap with their wings, to protect themselves, even if sick; birds commonly have parasites (fleas, lice, ticks) and carry diseases.
3. **Cover the bird with a light sheet or towel.**
4. **Gently pick up the bird and put it in the prepared container.**
5. **Warm the animal if it's cold out or if the animal is chilled.** Put <u>one end</u> of the animal's container on a heating pad set on low. Or fill a zip-top plastic bag, plastic soft drink container with a screw lid, or a rubber glove with hot water; wrap the warm container with cloth, and put next to the animal. Make sure the container doesn't leak, or the animal will get wet and chilled.
6. **Tape the box shut or roll the top of the paper bag closed.**
7. **Note exactly where you found the bird.** This will be very important for release.
8. **Keep the bird in a warm, dark, quiet place.**
   Don't give the bird food or water.
   Leave the bird alone; don't handle or bother it.
   Keep children and pets away.
9. **Contact a wildlife rehabilitator, state wildlife agency, or wildlife veterinarian as soon as possible.**
   Don't keep the bird at your home longer than necessary.
   Keep the bird in a container; don't let it loose in your house or car.
10. **Wash your hands after contact with the bird.**
    Wash anything the bird was in contact with — towel, jacket, blanket, pet carrier — to prevent the spread of diseases and/or parasites to you or your pets.
11. **Get the bird to a wildlife rehabilitator as soon as possible.**

Chapter 21

I Found a Baby Mammal ... *Now What?*

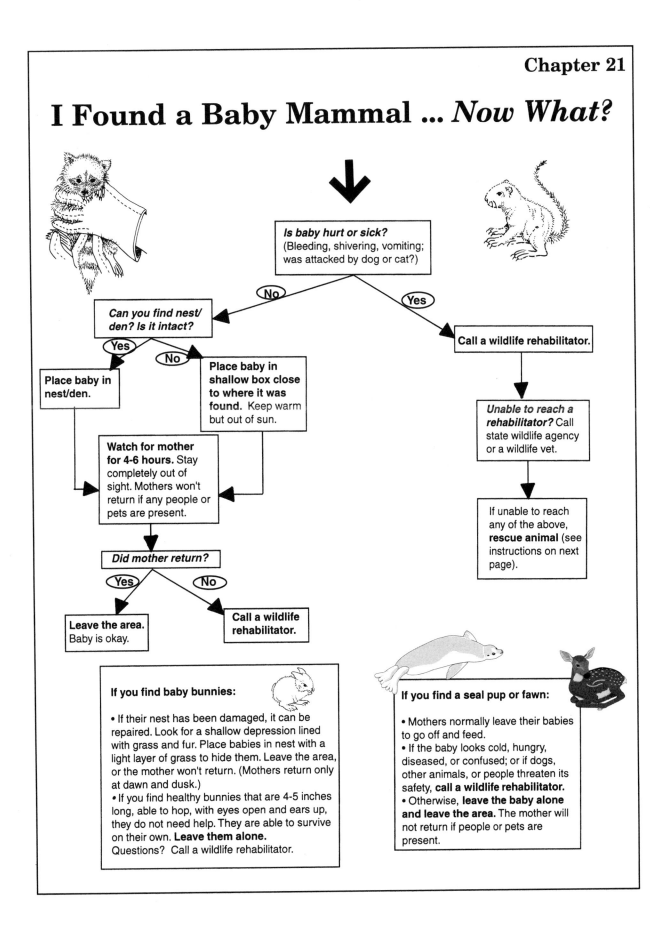

Is baby hurt or sick? (Bleeding, shivering, vomiting; was attacked by dog or cat?)

No → **Can you find nest/den? Is it intact?**

Yes → **Place baby in nest/den.**

No → **Place baby in shallow box close to where it was found.** Keep warm but out of sun.

Watch for mother for 4-6 hours. Stay completely out of sight. Mothers won't return if any people or pets are present.

Did mother return?

Yes → **Leave the area.** Baby is okay.

No → **Call a wildlife rehabilitator.**

Yes → **Call a wildlife rehabilitator.**

Unable to reach a rehabilitator? Call state wildlife agency or a wildlife vet.

If unable to reach any of the above, **rescue animal** (see instructions on next page).

If you find baby bunnies:

• If their nest has been damaged, it can be repaired. Look for a shallow depression lined with grass and fur. Place babies in nest with a light layer of grass to hide them. Leave the area, or the mother won't return. (Mothers return only at dawn and dusk.)
• If you find healthy bunnies that are 4-5 inches long, able to hop, with eyes open and ears up, they do not need help. They are able to survive on their own. **Leave them alone.**
Questions? Call a wildlife rehabilitator.

If you find a seal pup or fawn:

• Mothers normally leave their babies to go off and feed.
• If the baby looks cold, hungry, diseased, or confused; or if dogs, other animals, or people threaten its safety, **call a wildlife rehabilitator.**
• Otherwise, **leave the baby alone and leave the area.** The mother will not return if people or pets are present.

How to Rescue Baby Mammals

(Only adults should rescue baby mammals. Before rescuing adult mammals, seek guidance from a wildlife rehabilitator.)

1. **Prepare a container.** Place a soft cloth on the bottom of a cardboard box or cat/dog carrier with a lid. If it doesn't have air holes, make some. For smaller animals, you can use a paper sack with air holes punched in.
2. **Protect yourself.** Wear gloves, if possible. Some animals may bite or scratch to protect themselves, even if sick; wild animals commonly have parasites (fleas, lice, ticks) and carry diseases.
3. **Cover the animal with a light sheet or towel.**
4. **Gently pick up the animal and put it in the prepared container.**
5. **Warm the animal if it's cold out or if the animal is chilled.** Put <u>one end</u> of the container on a heating pad set on low. Or fill a zip-top plastic bag, plastic soft drink container with a screw lid, or a rubber glove with hot water; wrap warm container with cloth, and put it next to the animal. Make sure the container doesn't leak, or the animal will get wet and chilled.
6. **Tape the box shut or roll the top of the paper bag closed.**
7. **Note exactly where you found the animal.** This will be very important for release.
8. **Keep the animal in a warm, dark, quiet place.**
   Don't give it food or water.
   Leave it alone; don't handle or bother it.
   Keep children and pets away.
9. **Contact a wildlife rehabilitator, state wildlife agency, or wildlife veterinarian as soon as possible.**
   Don't keep the animal at your home longer than necessary.
   Keep the animal in a container; don't let it loose in your house or car.
10. **Wash your hands after contact with the animal.**
    Wash anything the animal was in contact with — towel, jacket, blanket, pet carrier — to prevent the spread of diseases and/or parasites to you or your pets.
11. **Get the animal to a wildlife rehabilitator as soon as possible.**

Chapter 22

Helping Marine Animals

Who Should Help?

Only experts should assist or rescue marine animals. The animals have very special needs, and they are too unpredictable for untrained people to manage.

If you see an orphaned, stranded, injured, or dead marine animal (manatee, dolphin, whale, sea turtle, seal, sea lion, or otter), *an adult should call the state Marine Patrol or Coast Guard right away.*

What to Report to Officials

- *What* you saw (species and size)
- *When* you saw it (time of day)
- *Where* it was located
- *How* it appeared (stranded, injured)

Dead marine animals should also be reported so biologists can check on the cause and, possibly, prevent more deaths.

For More Information

Photo: Critter Alley

Hanging in There.

State Wildlife Agencies

(Most numbers listed for rehabilitators are from 1996)

ALABAMA
Department of Conservation
and Natural Resources
Game & Fish/Wildlife Section
64 North Union St.
Montgomery, AL 36130
(334) 242-3469
rehabbers = 5 (estimated)
state license not required

ALASKA
Department of Fish & Game
Division of Wildlife
Conservation
P.O. Box 25526
Juneau, AK 99802
(907) 465-4190
rehabbers = 2 (raptor)
* *doesn't license mammal rehab*

ARIZONA
Arizona Game and Fish Dept.
2221 West Greenway Rd.
Phoenix, AZ 85023
(602) 582-9806
rehabbers = 55

ARKANSAS
Arkansas Game & Fish
Commission
Nongame Section
Rt 1 Box 188-A
Humphrey, AR 72073
(501) 873-4651
rehabbers = 31

CALIFORNIA
State of California
Dept. of Fish and Game
1416 Ninth St.
Sacramento, CA 95814
(916) 653-7664
rehabbers = about 87 licensed
centers, 11 licensed individuals

COLORADO
State of Colorado
Dept. of Natural Resources
Division of Wildlife
6060 Broadway
Denver, CO 80216-1000
(303) 297-1192
rehabbers = 60

CONNECTICUT
State of Connecticut
Department of Environmental
Protection
Wildlife Division
79 Elm St.
Hartford, CT 06106
(860) 424-3011
rehabbers = 191

DELAWARE
State of Delaware
Division of Fish and Wildlife
89 Kings Highway
P.O. Box 1401
Dover, DE 19903
(302) 739-5297
rehabbers = 2

FLORIDA
State of Florida
Game and Fresh Water Fish
Commission
Farris Bryant Building
Tallahassee, FL 32299-1600
(904) 488-4676
rehabbers = 320

GEORGIA
Georgia Dept. of Natural
Resources
Wildlife Resources Division
Special Permit Unit
2070 U.S. Highway 278, S.E.
Social Circle, GA 30279
(770) 918-6400
rehabbers = 262

HAWAII
State of Hawaii
Dept. of Land & Natural
Resources
Division of Forestry & Wildlife
1151 Punchbowl Street
Honolulu, HI 96813
(808) 587-0166
rehabbers = 15 (Oahu)

IDAHO
State of Idaho
Department of Game & Fish
600 S. Walnut St.
P.O. Box 25
Boise, ID 83707-0025
(208) 334-2920
rehabbers = 63

ILLINOIS
Illinois Department of
  Natural Resources
Division of Wildlife Resources
524 S. Second St.
Springfield, IL 62701-1787
(217) 782-6384
rehabbers = 310+

KANSAS
State of Kansas
Dept. Wildlife and Parks
Operations Office
512 SE 25th Avenue
Pratt, KS 67124-8174
(316) 672-5911
rehabbers = 72

MAINE
Maine Fish & Wildlife Dept.
284 State St.
Station 41
Augusta, ME 04333
(207) 289-2871
rehabbers = 110

MICHIGAN
State of Michigan
Dept. Natural Resources
Wildlife Division
P. O. Box 30444
Lansing, MI 48909-7944
(517) 373-1263
rehabbers = 165

MISSOURI
Missouri Department of
  Conservation
P.O. Box 180
Jefferson City, MO 65102-0180
(314) 751-4115
rehabbers = 31

INDIANA
State of Indiana
Division of Fish and Wildlife
402 W. Washington St.
Room W-273
Indianapolis, IN 46204
(317) 232-4080
rehabbers = 175

KENTUCKY
State of Kentucky
Dept. Fish & Wildlife Resources
#1 Game Farm Rd.
Frankfort, KY 40601
(502) 564-4406
rehabbers = 55

MARYLAND
State of Maryland
Dept. of Natural Resources
  Wildlife Division
580 Taylor Ave.
Annapolis, MD 21401
(410) 974-3195
rehabbers = 75

MINNESOTA
State of Minnesota
Dept. Natural Resources
Section of Wildlife
500 Lafayette Rd. Box 7
St. Paul, MN 55155-4007
(612) 296-3344
rehabbers = 150

MONTANA
Montana Department of Fish,
  Wildlife, and Parks
1420 E. Sixth Ave.
P.O. Box 200701
Helena, MT 59620
(406) 444-2535
rehabbers = 51

IOWA
Iowa Department of Natural
  Resources
Wallace State Office Building
Des Moines, IA 50319-0034
(515) 281-5638
rehabbers = 60

LOUISIANA
Dept. of Wildlife & Fisheries
Louisiana Natural Heritage
  Program
P.O. Box 98000
Baton Rouge, LA 70898-9000
(504) 765-2821
rehabbers = 33

MASSACHUSETTS
State of Massachusetts
Division of Fisheries & Wildlife
Leverett Saltonstall Bldg.
100 Cambridge St.
Boston, MA 02202
(617) 727-3151
rehabbers = 108

MISSISSIPPI
State of Mississippi
Department of Wildlife,
  Fisheries & Parks
P.O. Box 451
Jackson, MS 39205-0451
(601) 362-9212
rehabbers = 6

NEBRASKA
Nebraska Game and Parks
  Commission
P.O. Box 30370
Lincoln, NE 68503-0370
(402) 471-0641
rehabbers = 2

NEVADA
Nevada Division of Wildlife
P.O. Box 10678
Reno, NV 89520-0022
(702) 688-1500
rehabbers = 4

NEW MEXICO
New Mexico Dept. of Game
    and Fish
Villagra Building
Santa Fe, NM 87503
(505) 827-7897
rehabbers = 27

NORTH DAKOTA
Board of Animal Health
600 E. Blvd. Avenue
6th Floor
Bismarck, ND 58505
(701) 328-2654
rehabbers = 2
State wildlife agency does not handle

OREGON
Oregon Dept. Fish & Wildlife
Wildlife Division
2501 SW First Ave. PO Box 59
Portland, OR 97207
(503) 872-5260
rehabbers = 232

SOUTH CAROLINA
South Carolina Department
    of Natural Resources
P.O. Box 167/1000 Assembly St.
Columbia, SC 29202
(803) 734-3893
rehabbers = 68

NEW HAMPSHIRE
New Hampshire Fish and
    Game
2 Hazen Drive
Concord, NH 03301
(603) 271-3421
rehabbers = 30

NEW YORK
New York State
Dept. Environmental
    Conservation
50 Wolf Road
Albany, NY 12233-4752
(518) 457-0689
rehabbers - 680

OHIO
Department of Natural
    Resources
Division of Wildlife
1840 Belcher Drive
Columbus, OH 43224-1329
(614) 265-6338
rehabbers = 100

PENNSYLVANIA
Pennsylvania Game
    Commission
2001 Elmerton Avenue
Harrisburg, PA 17110-9797
(717) 783-8164
rehabbers = 53

SOUTH DAKOTA
South Dakota Department of
    Game, Fish & Parks
Foss Bldg
523 E. Capitol
Pierre, SD 57501-3182
(605) 773-3485
rehabbers = 6

NEW JERSEY
State of New Jersey
Dept. Environmental Protect.
Div. of Fish, Game & Wildlife
CN 400
Trenton, NJ 08625
(609)292-2965
rehabbers = 130

NORTH CAROLINA
North Carolina Wildlife
    Resources Commission
Nongame Division
512 N. Salisbury St.
Raleigh, NC 27602-1188
(919) 661-4872
rehabbers = about 300

OKLAHOMA
Oklahoma Department of
    Wildlife Conservation
1801 N. Lincoln Blvd.
Oklahoma City, OK 73105
(405) 521-3851
rehabbers = 77

RHODE ISLAND
State of Rhode Island
Dept. of Environmental Mgm.
Div. Fish & Wildlife/ Box 218
West Kingston, RI 02892
(401) 277-1267
rehabbers = 35

TENNESSEE
Tennessee Wildlife Resources
Ellington Agricultural Ctr.
P.O. Box 40747
Nashville, TN 37204-9979
(615) 781-6647
rehabbers = 80

191

TEXAS
Texas Parks and Wildlife Dept.
4200 Smith School Road
Austin, TX 78744
(512) 389-4481
rehabbers = 348

VIRGINIA
Commonwealth of Virginia
Dept. Game & Inland Fisheries
P.O. Box 11104
4010 W. Broad St.
Richmond, VA 23230-1104
(804) 367-1000
rehabbers = 238

WISCONSIN
Wisconsin Dept. of Natural
   Resources/ Bureau of
Wildlife Management
101 S. Webster/ Box 7921
Madison, WI 53707-7921
(608) 267-7507
rehabbers = 260

UTAH
State of Utah
Dept. of Natural Resources
Division of Wildlife Resources
1596 West North Temple
Salt Lake City, UT 84116-3195
(801) 538-4700
rehabbers = 14

WASHINGTON
State of Washington
Dept. of Fish and Wildlife
Wildlife Management
600 Capital Way N.
Olympia, WA 98501-1091
(360) 902-2515
rehabbers = 69

WYOMING
Wyoming Game and Fish Dept.
Wildlife Division
3400 Bishop Blvd.
Cheyenne, WY 82006
(307) 777-4600
rehabbers = 13

VERMONT
Vermont Natural Resources
Dept. Fish and Wildlife
103 South Main St., 10 South
Waterbury, VT 05671-0501
(802) 241-3700
rehabbers = 15

WEST VIRGINIA
West Virginia Division of
   Natural Resources/ Wildlife
Resources/ P.O. Box 67
Ward Road RTS 219/250 S
Elkins, WV 26241
(304) 637-0245
rehabbers = 3 (federal
   permits)
state license not required

U.S. Fish and Wildlife Service Regional Offices

Contact this government service about migratory birds or endangered species.

REGION 1 - PACIFIC (California, Hawaii, Idaho, Nevada, Oregon, Washington)
U.S. Fish and Wildlife Service
911 NE 11 Avenue
Portland, OR 97232-4181
(503) 231-6118

REGION 2 - SOUTHWEST (Arizona, New Mexico, Oklahoma, Texas)
U.S. Fish and Wildlife Service
P.O. Box 1306
Albuquerque, NM 87103
(505) 766-2321

REGION 3 - GREAT LAKES - BIG RIVERS
(Illinois, Indiana, Iowa, Michigan, Minnesota, Missouri, Ohio, Wisconsin)
U.S. Fish and Wildlife Service
1 Federal Drive
Fort Snelling, MN 55111-4056
(612) 725-3500

REGION 4 - SOUTHEAST (Alabama, Arkansas, Florida, Georgia, Kentucky, Louisiana, Mississippi, North Carolina, South Carolina, Tennessee)
U.S. Fish and Wildlife Service
1875 Century Blvd.
Atlanta, GA 30345
(404) 679-7319

REGION 5 - NORTHEAST
(Connecticut, D.C., Delaware, Maine, Maryland, Massachusetts, New Hampshire, New Jersey, New York, Pennsylvania, Rhode Island, Vermont, Virginia, West Virginia)
U.S. Fish and Wildlife Service
300 Westgate Center Drive
Hadley, MA 01035-9589
(413) 253-8200

REGION 6 - MOUNTAIN-PRAIRIE
(Colorado, Kansas, Montana, Nebraska, North Dakota, South Dakota, Utah, Wyoming)
U.S. Fish and Wildlife Service
P.O. Box 25486
Denver, CO 80025
(303) 236-7917

REGION 7 - ALASKA
U.S. Fish and Wildlife Service
1011 East Tudor Road
Anchorage, AK 99503
(907) 786-3542

Professional Wildlife Rehabilitation Organizations

National Wildlife Rehabilitators Association (NWRA)
14 North 7 Avenue
St. Cloud, MN 56303-4766
(320) 259-4086
Annual membership: $30 for individual

International Wildlife Rehabilitation Council (IWRC)
4437 Central Place
Suite B-4
Suisun, CA 94585
(707) 864-1761
Annual membership: $38 for individual

NWRA and IWRC are two professional organizations for wildlife rehabilitators. They offer educational opportunities and help members network with each other and exchange information among themselves and with specialists in other fields. They also publish professional journals that keep members updated on workshops and conferences, procedures, new supplies and equipment, and current issues in wildlife rehabilitation.

An increasing number of states also are forming professional organizations for wildlife rehabilitators. These allow rehabilitators to network among themselves on a more local scale.

Books About Wildlife Rescue and Rehabilitation

Picture Books

The Birdman of St. Petersburg by Tom Shachtman, Macmillan Publishing Co., 1982.

Buddy the Eagle Who Thought He Was a People (coloring book) by Lena Taylor Cox, Alaska Raptor Rehabilitation Center, Sitka, AK (1-800-643-9425).

Eagle Dreams by Sheryl McFarland, Philomel Books, 1994.

Humphrey the Lost Whale by Wendy Tokuda, Heian International, Inc., 1986.

Orphans from the Sea by Jack Denton Scott, Putnam, 1982.

Raptor Rescue by Sylvia Johnson, Dutton Childrens' Books, 1995.

The Six Bridges of Humphrey the Whale by Toni Knapp, The Rockrimmon Press, Inc., 1989.

Washing the Willow Tree Loon by Jacqueline Briggs Martin, Simon & Schuster Books for Young Readers, 1995.

When Birds Get Hurt (coloring book) by Sandy Kincheloe, Alaska Raptor Rehabilitation Center, Sitka, AK (1-800-643-9425).

Wildlife Rehabilitation: A Coloring and Activity Book by Pat Oldham and Wildlife Rescue, Inc., of New Mexico, Horizon Communications, 1995.

Wildlife Rescue: The Work of Dr. Kathleen Ramsay by Jennifer Owings Dewey, Boyd Mills Press, 1994.

Winter's Orphans by Robert C. Farentinos, Roberts Rinehart Publishers, 1993.

Books for Young Adults and Adults

All Wild Creatures Welcome by Patricia Curtis, E.P. Dutton, 1985.

The Avian Ark by Kit Chubb, Hungry Mind Press, 1991.

The Bat in My Pocket by Amanda Lollar, Capra Press, 1995.

Care of the Wild by W.J. Jordan and John Hughes, Rawson Associates, 1983.

For the Love of Wild Things by Mary Jane Stretch and Phyllis Hobe, Stackpole Books, 1995.

Into the Blue by Virginia McKenna, HarperSanFrancisco, 1992.

Living with Wildlife by The California Center for Wildlife, Sierra Club Books, 1994.

My Orphans of the Wild by Rosemary Collett, J.B. Lippincott Company, 1974.

Books for Young Adults and Adults (cont.)

A Place for Owls by Katherine McKeever, Firefly Books, 1992.
A Seal Called Andre by Harry Goodridge and Lew Dietz, Down East Books, 1975.
Wild Neighbors, The Humane Approach to Living with Wildlife, The Humane Society of the United States, Fulcrum Publishing, 1997.
Wildlife Rescue by Barbara Ford and Stephen Ross, Albert Whiteman & Company, 1987.

Videos

"Andre," movie and video, 1994.
"Fly Away Home," movie and video, 1996.
"Free Willy," movie and video, 1993.
"Free Willy 2," movie and video, 1995.
"A Home for Pearl," four-part video (70 minutes) & Instructional Guide for elementary school children teaches about wildlife habitat, what wildlife need to survive, difference between wild and domestic animals, predators, endangered species, and the effects of habitat loss. © 1990 National Fish and Wildlife Foundation.

> Contact: U.S. Fish and Wildlife Service
> Publications Unit, Arlington Square
> 849 C Street NW, Washington, DC 20240.

"Release," exciting 24-minute video documenting first all-volunteer U.S. whale rescue, rehabilitation, and release coordinated by two (noncaptive) marine mammal/wildlife rescue organizations (as described in Chapter 15 of this book).

> Contact: Marine Mammal Conservancy
> Box 1625 Key Largo, FL 33037
> (305) 853-0675

Magazine

Wildlife Rehabilitation Today
Coconut Creek Publishing Company
2300 West Sample Road, Suite 314
Pompano Beach, FL 33073-3046
(954) 977-5058

Subscription: $15 per year (published quarterly)

Wild Again

by Douglas Wood

1. I came on my sister alone and afraid
   It seems that she fell from the sky.
   The gift that had carried her into the clouds,
   Now was gone and she couldn't know why.

   She'd sailed like a ship upon oceans of air,
   As wild and as free as the wind,
   But something had taken her out of the sky
   And now here to the earth she was pinned.

   Come with me, my love, and we'll do what we can
   To set right what has somehow gone wrong.
   We'll work with the feather and sinew and bone,
   To give back to your spirit its song. CHORUS

2. I came on my brother, so tiny and weak
   He couldn't yet care for himself.
   Somehow he'd been left alone in the world
   And to make it he needed some help.

   Something had taken his mother away,
   A highway, a trap, or a storm.
   He needed a chance to become who he was,
   To be sheltered and fed and kept warm.

   Come with me, my friend, and we'll do what we can
   To set right what has somehow gone wrong.
   We'll try hard to raise you the wild thing you are
   And give back to your spirit its song. CHORUS

CHORUS
And you'll feel once more the wind in your wings,
Or climb where the tall mountains stand.
You'll run the wide prairie
Or haunt the dark forest,
My friend, you will be wild again.
My friend, you will be wild again.

---

3. With our brothers and sisters we all share one world
   And there's one common spirit within.
   It's the wild things that help us survive on this earth
   Without them we couldn't begin.

   So once in awhile we've a chance to give back
   Just a little from all that we take.
   And a wild one returned to the circle of life
   Is a part of the world that we make.

   And we'll feel once more the wind in our wings
   Or climb where the tall mountains stand.
   We'll run the wide prairie
   Or haunt the dark forest,
   My friends, we will be wild again.
   My friends, we will be wild again. CHORUS

This song was commissioned by the National Wildlife Rehabilitators Association (NWRA) in 1984. Douglas Wood is a songwriter from Minnesota and the author of *Old Turtle*. To order an audiotape of Doug singing "Wild Again," contact: National Wildlife Rehabilitators Association
14 North 7 Avenue
St. Cloud, MN 56303-4766
(320) 259-4086

GLOSSARY

A

algae (AL gee) — tiny floating plants that grow in water. High concentrations of blooming *algae* in the ocean cause a condition known as "red tide."

anesthesia (AN es THEE shuh) — medicine that puts patients to sleep during surgery. Doing surgery on dolphins is risky because they stop breathing if they receive *anesthesia.*

aviary (AA vee air ee) — a large enclosure for birds. A bird being rehabilitated is moved to an *aviary* when it's well enough to fly.

B

beached — to be stuck in sand or shallow water on shore. Humphrey, a humpback whale, *beached* in a river of shallow water.

biology — the study of all life forms.

birds of prey — (also known as *raptors*) birds that hunt other animals for food. *Birds of prey* use sharp talons to capture and kill prey and hooked beaks to tear the meat.

blind — a hiding place for observing or hunting wildlife. One rehabilitator used her car as a *blind* when watching a barn owl nest.

blowhole — a nostril (or two) in the top of whales' or dolphins' heads. When a dolphin surfaces, it exhales, spraying water through its *blowhole,* before it inhales.

blubber — fat. Most marine mammals have a lot of *blubber* to protect them from cold water.

buoyant (BOY unt) — able to float. Because whales are *buoyant,* their massive weight is held up by the water.

C

captive breeding — the breeding of wild animals in captivity. *Captive breeding* has helped increase the numbers of black-footed ferrets, which are among the most endangered mammals on earth.

carnivores (CAR nuh vorz) — primarily meat eaters. Cougars and birds of prey are *carnivores.*

carrion (CARRY un) — dead animals. Vultures do us a favor by eating *carrion,* especially alongside roads.

cetacean (suh TAY shun) — marine mammals that include whales, dolphins, and porpoises. *Cetaceans* are very intelligent animals with strong family bonds.

confiscate (CON fuh skate) — to take away, especially by law enforcement officials. Sometimes rehabilitators receive free meat when wildlife officials *confiscate* illegally killed animals from poachers.

conscious breathing (KON shus breathing) — nonautomatic breathing that requires part of the brain to stay awake. Because of *conscious breathing,* cetaceans never sleep deeply.

crepuscular (cruh PUS cue lur) — active mostly at dawn and dusk. Deer and rabbits are *crepuscular* creatures.

D

dehydration (de HI drayt ud) — loss of body fluids. *Dehydration* is a problem with many sick animals because they're too sick to eat or drink.

den — to sleep for the winter. Bears *den* in logs or caves.

dental acrylic (dental ah CRILL ick) — substance used by dentists on human teeth because it hardens when mixed correctly. Sometimes *dental acrylic* is used to repair cracked turtle shells.

development — the clearing of land for homes, businesses, or agriculture. *Development* destroys wildlife habitats everywhere.

displace — to force out. Our new homes, schools, and roads often *displace* wildlife.

diurnal (DIE urn ul) — active during the daytime. With the exception of owls, birds of prey are *diurnal* hunters.

domestic (doe MESS tik) — tame animals that live safely with or around people. Cats and dogs are *domestic* animals.

domesticate (doe MESS ta KATE) — to tame wild animals. It took tens of thousands of years to *domesticate* wolves into the dogs we know today.

down — fuzzy, fluffy feathers. Nestling birds may be naked or covered with *down*.

E

ecology (e CALL ah gee) — study of the relationship among plants, animals, and their habitats.

endangered species (in DANE jerd SPEE cees) — in danger of becoming extinct. Because there are only about 2,000 manatees left in the wild, they are considered *endangered*.

extinction (ek STINK shun) — death of all the animals in a species, which will never exist again. The *extinction* of any species is a loss to all life.

euthanasia (YOU thun A juh) — the humane killing of sick or injured animals as an act of mercy or compassion. *Euthanasia* is a necessary part of wildlife rehabilitation.

F

fledgling (FLEJ ling) — young birds learning to fly. *Fledglings* are sometimes called "branchers," because they perch on branches near their nest.

flight cage — an enclosure large enough for birds to practice flying. Birds of Prey Rehabilitation Foundation in Broomfield, Colorado, has some of the largest *flight cages* in the U.S.

flyways — frequently traveled paths of migrating birds. The Pacific, Central, Mississippi, and Atlantic are the main *flyways* in the U.S.

foot — to stab with talons (claws). When rescuing raptors, you need to be careful to hold the birds' feet, or they may *foot* you.

forage (FOR ij) — to search for food. Wild animal parents teach their young where to *forage* for foods.

formula — a substitute milk mixture for baby animals. Different species of animals require different *formulas*.

foster parents — animals usually of the same species that take care of orphaned babies. Male and female animals make good *foster parents*.

freeze brand — a painless mark made on marine animals for identification. Previously rehabilitated dolphins in the wild are identified by *freeze brands*.

G

gaping — opening the mouth for food. *Gaping* baby birds get fed by their parents.

gosling — baby goose

groom — to clean feathers or fur. Animals *groom* themselves to keep their fur waterproof and to keep their feathers waterproof and working perfectly for flight.

H

habitat (HA buh tat) — places where animals live naturally. A *habitat* provides food, water, space, and shelter.

haul-out areas — places where marine animals can climb out of the water. Floating docks at PIER 39 in San Francisco's Fisherman's Wharf are *haul-out areas* for sea lions.

herpetology (HERP uh TALL uh gee) — the study of reptiles and amphibians. Some rehabilitators study *herpetology* so they can treat snakes, frogs, and lizards.

hibernate (HI burr nayte) — to sleep through the winter. Groundhogs are the best known animals that *hibernate*.

humane (hew MANE) — kind or compassionate. *Humane* treatment of all life is important.

hypothermia (HI po THERM ee ah) — low body temperature. Without blubber or fur, marine mammals would develop *hypothermia* from cold sea water.

I

immune (ee MEWN) — protected from something, such as a disease. Rehabilitators who work with bats get rabies shots so they'll be *immune* to rabies.

imprint (IM print) — when baby animals identify with their mothers and believe they are the same species. Baby geese *imprint* on the first creature they see.

incubator (INK you bay tur) — an enclosure for baby animals with controlled heat and humidity. Naked nestling birds have to stay in *incubators* for warmth.

instinct (IN stinkt) — an animal's automatic response to something in its environment. A mother bear's *instinct* is to fight to protect her young.

intravenous (IN trah VEEN us) — given through a needle into the vein. *Intravenous* fluids and medicines are given to very sick animals that can't eat.

J

jesses — short leather straps around the legs of raptors used for catching the birds and attaching leashes. Education raptors wear *jesses* in the classroom so they can be kept on a glove or stand.

L

locks — enclosures (as in canals) with gates at each end, used to raise boats as they pass from level to level. Some manatees are crushed when passing through *locks*.

M

maggots — fly larvae (grubs). Sometimes rehabilitators have to pick *maggots* out of animals' wounds.

mange (maynj) — skin disease with itching and loss of hair, caused by a tiny parasite. Foxes can spread *mange* to people's pets and to people.

manning – training. *Manning* raptors for education birds takes a lot of time and patience.

marine — pertaining to the sea. Most *marine* mammals spend all their time in the sea.

marsupial (mar SOUP ee ul) — an order of mammals in which females carry their young in a pouch. Opossums are the only *marsupials* native to North America.

mature (ma CHURE) — to become fully grown and developed. *Mature* bald eagles have white feathers on their heads.

mealworms — beetle larvae, used to feed insect-eating birds and mammals. *Mealworms* often are raised in rehabilitation centers and used for wildlife food.

migrate (MY grayt) — to travel seasonally from one territory to another for feeding and breeding. Many of our birds *migrate* to Central and South America.

mites (mytz) — tiny parasites that burrow under an animal's skin, causing itching, hair loss, and sometimes, death. If infected with *mites*, animals can spread them, even in people's homes.

molt — to shed fur or feathers

N

native — living or growing naturally in a place. *Native* animals often have no defenses against introduced animals such as cats and rats.

natural history — the habits, biology, and needs of wildlife. Knowing the *natural history* of wildlife is very important when caring for them.

necropsy (NECK ropp see) — medical examination of a dead animal. *Necropsies* were done on dead manatees to help scientists figure out what caused the massive die-off in 1996.

nestling — a young bird still in the nest. A *nestling* may be naked or it may have some feathers, but it can't fly.

nocturnal (nock TURN uhl) — active at night. Owls are *nocturnal* birds.

O

ornithology — the study of birds. Some rehabilitators are very knowledgeable about *ornithology*.

owl pellets — the undigestible parts of prey that owls spit up. If you look beneath trees where owls roost, you'll probably find *owl pellets*.

P

parasite (PEAR ah site) — an organism that lives in or on another organism. Wild animals often have *parasites*, such as intestinal worms, and some can be passed to pets or people.

peninsula (pen IN sue la) — land nearly surrounded by water and connected to the mainland by a narrow strip of land. Cape Cod is a *peninsula*.

pinky — a hairless, pink, deaf and blind newborn mammal. A *pinky* will die quickly without warmth.

poach — to hunt or trap illegally. We all need to report people that *poach* wildlife.

post-release study — research done on wildlife after release from rehabilitation centers, to check how they are doing. *Post-release studies* on rehabilitated black bear cubs show that they tend to stay far away from people.

preen — to comb or clean feathers with a beak or bill. Birds *preen* frequently to keep their feathers clean and straight.

predator (PRED ah tur) — an animal that hunts and eats other animals. Raptors are *predators*.

prey — an animal that is hunted and eaten by a predator. Rodents are common *prey* for raptors.

Q

quarantine (KWOR un teen) — isolation from other creatures for a period of time. Newly admitted animals are often put in *quarantine* to protect the other animals.

R

raptors (RAP tur) — birds of prey. *Raptors* are fascinating birds that help people by eating many rodents and insects.

rabies (RAY beez) — a viral disease transmitted by bites, scratches, or saliva from an infected animal. Without treatment, *rabies* is fatal.

rabies vector species — animals that most commonly carry and spread rabies. *Rabies vector species* usually include skunks, raccoons, bats, foxes, and coyotes.

red tide — discolored seawater caused by blooming algae. *Red tide* in high concentrations is toxic to fish and many marine animals.

regenerate (ree JEN ur ate) — to grow back or heal. The injured tissue in a cracked turtle shell will *regenerate* in time if the turtle gets good medical treatment.

regurgitate (ree GURGE ah tate) — to throw up partially digested food. Some bird parents *regurgitate* food to feed their babies.

rehabilitate (ree ha BILL uh tate) — to restore to health. It's wonderful to know that there are people who care enough to *rehabilitate* sick, injured, or orphaned wildlife.

roost — to rest or sleep. Birds often *roost* in trees.

S

socialized — to become used to a person or another animal. If handled too much, wild animals can become *socialized* to humans, losing their protective fear.

species (SPEE ceez) — animals that look alike and can breed among themselves. There are nearly 1,000 different *species* of bats in the world.

strand — when marine animals go ashore or stay in shallow water where they wouldn't normally be, and they seem in distress. Usually, marine animals are sick or injured when they *strand*.

subcutaneous (sub cue TANE ee us) — delivered under the skin. Wildlife may receive *subcutaneous* fluids if they can't eat or drink.

surrogate (SIR uh gut) — a substitute. Sometimes, rehabilitators use puppets or stuffed animals as *surrogate* mothers for orphaned animals.

T

talons — sharp, curved claws. Raptors use their *talons* to catch prey.

threatened species — species whose numbers have decreased dangerously but are not considered endangered. Brown pelicans are a *threatened species*.

tote — an enclosure with water. A rehabilitating otter swims in a portable *tote*.

toxic — poisonous. Oil is *toxic* to wildlife and people.

tube-feed — to pass a narrow tube from an animal's mouth into its stomach in order to give it food, fluids, or medications. Rehabilitators sometimes *tube-feed* baby opossums.

V

ventilator — a machine that breathes for patients during surgery. Whales need to be on *ventilators* if they receive anesthesia.

veterinary technician (VET er in AIR ee tek NISH un) — a licensed professional who is a veterinary assistant, much like an animal care nurse. Some wildlife rehabilitators are *veterinary technicians*.

vixen — a female fox. A *vixen* teaches her young how to hunt and avoid humans.

W

weaned — not nursing anymore. A young animal needs to find its own food if it's *weaned*.

wildlife rehabilitators — people who take care of orphaned, sick, or injured wildlife, with the purpose of restoring them to health and returning them to the wild. *Wildlife rehabilitators* have a lot of knowledge about wildlife injuries, diseases, and treatments.

Z

zoology — study of the biology of animals. Many rehabilitators study *zoology* to learn as much as possible about wildlife.

zoonoses — diseases passed from wildlife to people. Some *zoonoses* can be very dangerous, even fatal, for humans.

Contributing Illustrators

Donna Clement (Longmont, Colorado) has volunteered at Birds of Prey Foundation in Broomfield, Colorado, for many years. She's been involved in many aspects of the organization, including giving injured raptors a ride to the Foundation, when called on. Donna is at her best providing beautiful pen and ink illustrations of Colorado's birds of prey. The Foundation has used Donna's artwork on T-shirts, brochures, and in educational materials. Donna also designs and paints the sets for a local theater and does a variety of free-lance work, including theatrical murals, illustrations, and portraits in the Denver-Boulder area.

Paula Nicholas (Denver, Colorado) has worked for 27 years as a scientific illustrator, completing biological, botanical, environmental, and medical artwork for various purposes. Originally from southern California, she has lived and worked in Colorado since 1977. Paula has a broad educational background in science and has earned her M.S. from Colorado State University in Fort Collins. She also has had many other varied work experiences, including environmental consulting, scientific researcher, grant writer, and science and illustration teacher positions.

Contributing Photographers

Susan Ahalt (Cody, Wyoming) is director of Ironside Bird Rescue.

Luanne Albright (Epping, New Hampshire) is a wildlife rehabilitator licensed in the state of New Hampshire, specializing in bats.

Stanley B. Ashbrook (Largo, Florida) has been a dedicated amateur nature photographer for over 40 years. His photos have appeared in newspapers, books, and magazines, including *National Wildlife* and *Guidepost*.

Ken Bach (San Raton, California) has been with The Marine Mammal Center in Sausalito, California, for nine years, taking care of photographs for about seven. For 14 years, he's worked for Ilufuro Photo. Photography and animals have been part of his life since he started an animal shelter in 1975 and was the photo editor for his high school year book in 1977.

Caroline Brawner (Santa Fe, New Mexico) volunteered at The Marine Mammal Center in Sausalito, California, from 1984-1986.

Shannon Brink (Denver, Colorado), age ten, enjoys photography, soccer, and reading.

Dr. Helen Connor (Tuscalossa, Alabama), a professor emeritus at the University of Alabama, was a volunteer with Alabama Wildlife Rehabilitation Center and librarian, among other varied activities (1986-1991).

Gary Crandall (Salt Lake City, Utah) has owned and operated Dancing Crane Productions since 1991. It features his hauntingly beautiful wildlife photography, which depicts animals in their natural habitats, undisturbed. None of the wildlife has been rented, baited, or harassed in any way. The cover photo he shot for this book is the first time Gary has included people with wildlife.

Contributing Photographers (cont.)

Greg Crenshaw was a volunteer for Alabama Wildlife Rehabilitation Center for three years, while living in Birmingham. He enjoyed any opportunity to capture wild patients on film. Greg now lives in NW Alabama, where he opened a studio for children's portraiture. He's now able to photograph wild creatures on a daily basis. He also continues to volunteer in the Shoals area.

Critter Alley (see Janet Walker)

Jonathan X. Di Cesare (Houston, Texas) is a part-time photographer specializing in wild animal/human interaction (usually wild animal rehabilitation). From New York State, Jonathan lives in Houston with his wife and son while completing graduate studies at Rice University. He would like to thank The Wildlife Center of Harris County Precinct 4 for their assistance in helping him pursue his photographic interests.

Coleen Doucette (Newark, Delaware) is a veterinary technician and wildlife rehabilitator working with Tri-State Bird Rescue and Research.

Greg Ewert (Lopez Island, Washington) is a teacher on Lopez. This year he is teaching a K-5 multigrade alternative classroom while pursuing his passion, photography, on the side. He is working with a writer and doing photographs and interviews of the people on Lopez.

Rosa and Dave Felder live in Broomfield, Colorado.

Tom Fell lives in Cody, Wyoming.

John Findlay III became known as "Mr. Bluebird" after starting a Bluebird Trail in Oak Mountain State Park (Alabama) in 1979. From seven boxes it expanded into 180 boxes, 100 of which were in the park and the others in Jefferson and Shelby Counties. Mr. Findlay was born and grew up in Wakefield, Massachusetts. He lived in Illinois for 28 years and in Birmingham, Alabama, for 18. Because of Mr. Findlay's work with bluebirds in the park, the main road was named The John Findlay III Road. He died in 1995.

Doug Franklin is an artist who lives in western Colorado.

Kari Gabriel lives in Kalispel, Montana.

Bobbi J. Geise is director of Bridger Outdoor Science School in Bozeman, Montana. Formerly, she was director of Big Sky Wildcare, a raptor rehabilitation facility.

Greenwood Wildlife Rehabilitation Sanctuary
5761 Highway 66
Longmont, CO 80503
(303) 545-5849

Kim Heacox (Gustavus, Alaska) has written and photographed several books on Alaska, including *In Denali* and *Alaska Light*.

Harvey and Pamela Hergett (Quincy, California) were volunteers at Alaska Raptor Rehabilitation Center from 1993-1996.

Catherine Hurlbutt (Denver, Colorado) has loved birds all of her 84 years. A government stenographer for 41 years, Catherine has also rescued and rehabilitated birds for many decades. She's written nine remarkable books about her experiences with birds.

George Jackson (Denver, Colorado) is president of Jackson Group International, an executive search company. He and his wife, Shannon Jacobs, enjoy traveling and photographing wildlife.

Diane Johnson (Linwood, Kansas) is a licensed registered veterinary technician who has worked for area veterinarians for 18 years. She is founder and director of OWL (Operation Wildlife), the largest wildlife rehabilitation center in the state of Kansas. In 1996 OWL volunteers admitted 2,881 animals and educated more than 260,000 people via programs and telephone hotlines. Diane is married and the mother of three children, ages 4, 7, and 15.

Michael Judish (Northglenn, Colorado) has taken stunning photographs of weather phenomena, dynamic landscapes, and wildlife for many years.

Contributing Photographers (cont.)

Amanda Lollar (Mineral Wells, Texas) is the author of *The Bat in My Pocket*. She's also a scientific wildlife rehabilitator and the director of Bat World Sanctuary in Mineral Wells.

Sally Maughan (Boise, Idaho) has been a wildlife rehabilitator for 19 years. She is the founder of Coyote Foster Parent Program and Idaho Black Bear Rehab., Inc.

David McCoy (Morristown, Tennessee) is a building designer, specializing in custom homes. A member of American Institute of Building Design, David has used his skills to design and build flight cages for his wife (and rehabilitator) Lynne. David also is a wildlife artist, as well as his wife's "right hand" in support of the wildlife work.

Lynne McCoy (Morristown, Tennessee) has been a wildlife rehabilitator for more than 20 years in East Tennessee. Lynne uses a Minolta Freedom Zoom camera and relies on 400 speed film and the trusty camera. "If I tried to manage f-stops, etc., my critters would be long gone!" she says. So she tries to "quick catch" personalities of her patients on film.

Jane Oka (Mill Valley, California) is a graphic designer and illustrator in the real world. But she cannot envision life without the rich experience and privileges working in close proximity with wildlife. Photography is Jane's creative extension at The Marine Mammal Center in Sausalito, California. Her participation in animal care began in 1979. She's been shift supervisor since 1983.

Rosemary Perfit lives in Tampa, Florida.

Phylis Rollins (Dandridge, Tennessee) spent many years in San Francisco Bay area rehabilitating wildlife and animals most people found boring — turtles, opossums, skunks — and discovered that the sweetest, most fascinating teachers in life are quite often those overlooked. She moved to the woodlands of East Tennessee to live a simpler lifestyle devoted to the land and wildlife. Besides rehabilitating, Phylis enjoys meditation, writing, and native crafts.

Cindy Rork (Denver, Colorado) is an elementary school teacher in Englewood, Colorado. She does several wildlife rescue projects with fourth-graders each year. Cindy has twin fifth-grade sons, Andrew and Chris.

Tom Sanders and his wife, Cec, have been married 25 years and wildlife rehabilitators for more than 20 years. They live at the base of Wet Mountain and operate Wet Mountain Wildlife Rehabilitation Center, a facility for helping the wildlife of Colorado.

Chris Schulz (Castle Hayne, North Carolina) is a volunteer with The Marine Mammal Conservancy in Key Largo and Wildlife Rescue of the Florida Keys. She's also a member of the Florida Keys Marine Mammal Rescue Team.

Wendy Shattil and Bob Rozinski (Denver, Colorado) are widely published professional nature and wildlife photographers noted for their behavioral and evocative images.

Paula Stolebarger lives and works in Denver, Colorado.

Amy Sweeney (Sitka, Alaska) is a volunteer and supporter of Alaska Raptor Rehabilitation Center. She has a home-based business, Sand Dollar Designs. Her specialty is Northern Lights photography, but she also does specialty printing/illustrations and graphic design.

Texas State Aquarium
  2710 N. Shoreline
  Corpus Christi, TX 78402
  (800) 477-GULF

Sigrid Ueblacker (Broomfield, Colorado) is the founder and director of Birds of Prey Foundation.

Contributing Photographers (cont.)

Urban Wildlife Rescue (Denver, Colorado) was formed by Jack and Penny Murphy in November, 1991. They rehabilitate 150-200 fur-bearing mammals annually. The animals range from bats to coyotes. Jack and Penny give 75-100 educational programs every year to schools, animal control agencies, and homeowner associations. Through Urban Wildlife Rescue's "Humane Solutions to Wildlife Problems," 3,000 citizens are helped with wildlife conflicts, either over the phone or with on-site assistance. More than 8,000 wild animals are saved each year because of this program.

Karen Von den Deale (Brewster, Massachusetts) has been a state and federally licensed wildlife rehabilitator since 1989. She founded WILD CARE, Inc., in 1994, when an "empty nest syndrome" led her back to her childhood love of nature — the wild outdoors and animals. WILD CARE admits about 1,400 birds, mammals, and reptiles annually, and the animals are treated with the highest professional standards. Karen remains an amateur photographer.

Janet Walker (Grand Ledge, Michigan) is a state and federally licensed wildlife rehabilitator who has been rehabilitating wildlife for over 20 years. She is the executive director of Critter Alley Wildlife Rehabilitation Center, one of the nation's largest and most comprehensive centers. She is a member of NWRA and IWRC and has been an invited speaker to numerous conferences. Over the years, Janet has received local and national acclaim for her work with wildlife, including the State of Michigan Special Tribute. She has been featured on CNN and has been written about in *Wildlife Rehabilitation Today* and other publications.

B.D. Wehrfritz (Meeteetse, Wyoming) is a professional wildlife nature photographer who volunteers photographic services for Ironside Bird Rescue in Cody, Wyoming.

W.E.R.C. : Wildlife Education & Rehabilitation Center
P.O. Box 1105
Morgan Hill, CA 95038
(408) 779-WERC

Index

Healers of the Wild

Book Order Form
ISBN# 0-9661070-0-4

Books: $19.95 each.. = _____

        Colorado residents add 7.3% sales tax ($1.46 per book) .... = _____

    • **If 2-5 books are ordered**, take 10% off each book = **$17.95** x _____books .... = _____

        Colorado residents add 7.3% sales tax ($1.31 per book)................................. = _____

    • **If more than 5 books are ordered,** take 20% off each book = **$15.96** x_____ books.......... = _____

        Colorado residents add 7.3% sales tax ($1.17 per book)................................. = _____

    • **If you are a wildlife rehabilitator,** take 30% off each book = **$13.96** x_____ books........... = _____

        Colorado residents (if not tax exempt), add 7.3% sales tax ($1.02 per book)......... = _____

Shipping and Handling: $2.00 per book x _____books .... = _____

                                        Total.................. = _____

Name_____Phone_____

Address_____City_____State_____Zip_____

Wildlife rehabilitators/volunteers, please list licensed center/individual_____

_____

If you would like your book autographed by the author, please print name to be inscribed:

Send check or money order payable to:

Coyote Moon Press
PO Box 6867
Denver, CO 80206

Call 303-316-4633 for questions
Fax: 303-321-3551

Donna Clement

For Icarus

Lovely Blue Falcon
who stayed for a year
I lost you forever
and wish you'd be here.

Children stopped playing
when he stood on my glove
listening to stories
of the birds I love.

Hawks with crushed wings
from gunshot and wire
they all came to me
exhausted and tired.

Satin winged Eagles
looking at me
stretching their wings
longing to be free.

Sweet little Kestrel
can't fly any more
waits to be mended
and the sky to soar.

Soft feathered Owls
with yellow eyes
dreaming of freedom
and the moon to rise.

Twelve different Hawks
sit side by side
telling me stories
of the thermals to ride.

Little lost Owl
can't yet go home
just wait a little longer
for the skies to roam.

Lovely Blue Falcon
I miss you all day
I lost you forever
and wish you'd have stayed!

Sigrid Ueblacker
Birds of Prey Foundation